CHURCH

Is There An App For That?

Exploring Aspects of Authentic Body Life

Dan Rutherford

Axiom Publishing House

Church: Is There An App For That?
Exploring Aspects of Authentic Body Life
Copyright © 2015 Dan Rutherford

ISBN-10: 1502937824

Cover Design - Trent Ottosen

Interior Design support - Amber Smart

Edited by: Robyn Olfert

Printed in the United States of America

Contents

Dedication

To my wonderful wife Beverly; our daughters Celeste and Karissa; my mother Joanne; my maternal grandmother Etta Doyle, who modeled a life of loving Jesus and others; and to our friend who preceded us to heaven, Rosie Mott M.D.

Special Thanks

Being a novice at writing a book has meant I have needed the help and support of a great variety of friends to help complete the project. Thank you for proof-reading, grammar help and editing to many folks, but especially the following: Jennifer Heller-Stohler, Elizabeth Honeycutt, Robyn Olfert, Celeste Rutherford, April Klassen, & Laura Van Leewen.

Also thank you to The Centre for the Study of Religion and Society (CSRS) at the University of Victoria for allowing me to complete Research Fellowship 2014 with access to resources for writing and collegiality.

Contact The Author & Join The Conversation:

https://www.facebook.com/ChurchAppBook

'All that is gold does not glitter.'

—Tolkien

Endorsements

"The prophets, though oft-times startling us with their searing vision of God, didn't traffic in theological novelties: they just relentlessly called us back to the bedrock, the ancient paths. In that sense, Dan's book is prophetic. It's a call for the church to be the church, and a vivid and wooing portrait of what that means. Only a seasoned pastor could have written this. Even more, only a lover of Christ's Bride could have written it."
Mark Buchanan – Best Selling Author and Pastor

"By almost every standard of assessment the Church in North America is seriously unwell. Dan Rutherford's wide-ranging chapters offer at many points both a credible diagnosis, as well as a thoughtful and accessible prescription for recovery. I commend it warmly."
Dr. Bruce Milne – Pastor and Best Selling Author of *Know The Truth*

"It has been said that the task of the Church is to be culturally engaged and morally distinct: alas too often we Christians are culturally disengaged and morally similar. It's time to do some deep thinking and not be afraid of asking ourselves some tough questions. Not shying away from difficult answers, Dan Rutherford's book helps Christians think through what it means to be Church in the fast moving, media saturated, digitally driven culture in which we find ourselves."
Dr. Andy Bannister - Canadian Director and Lead Apologist, Ravi Zacharias International Ministries

"Dan's book Church: *Is There an App for That?* is an inspiration to those of us who are called to an authentic walk with Jesus. The book serves as a reminder to what that should actually look like.

Marginal Christians and occasional church goers will find biblical evidence on the Holy Spirit-filled benefits of commitment and involvement in the church and ultimately an intimate relationship with God."

Walle Larsson – Jazz Musician Extraordinaire
www.wallelarsson.com

"People have a way of dressing up Christ's bride, the church, into something truly horrid that we either shriek at the sight of or avoid altogether. Dan's love for the church and desire to see her original grace-filled beauty lived out in the lives of men and women that love God and people make this book a must-read."

Andy Steiger - Director of Apologetics Canada

CHAPTER ONE

Not the Preface: nobody Reads That!

Applications - more commonly known as apps—are shortcuts designed for accomplishing specific tasks.[1] In less than a decade, some 1.5 million apps have been developed that enable users to accomplish almost every conceivable task, from finding movies, meals, and mates, to banking, or tracking. Whatever you can possibly imagine, there is an app for that. Harvard Magazine recently explored just how big an impact apps have had on our culture and on an emerging generation. "Young people growing up in our time are not only immersed in apps, they've come to think of the world as an ensemble of apps, to see their lives as a string of ordered apps, or perhaps, in many cases, a single, extended, cradle-to-grave app."[2] This world of apps seems to offer remarkable conveniences, yet the concern of some social scientists is that apps create a dependence that inhibits many in our culture from exploring solutions for themselves. They say, "The app mindset, motivates youth to seek direct, quick, easy solutions—the kinds of answers an app would provide—and to shy away from questions, whether large or small, when there's no 'app for that.' "[3]

What this book offers is a chance to explore for ourselves the topic of the Church while attempting to *not* offer simple and easy formulas. We may discover that many people in our culture have not so much rejected the church, as have rejected the poor caricatures of it. What is needed in our app culture is to explore some of the authentic depictions of what the Church is all about as found in the source material (the Bible) and what it means to be a part of it.

The Search Goes On

Recently I was at a coffee shop near my home, holding an open forum for those who want to ask questions about faith and Christianity. This informal gathering is held in order to shed some light on issues that have been keeping people from faith in Jesus; it is often quite lively! On this specific night, I was challenged by a very aggressive man about the church and its failures, and in particular, the way he had been hurt by a specific church.

Ironically, that same week I was processing my own wounds and sadness regarding my experience in ministry having recently endured some rather nasty politics of church life. Yet there I was defending the historic church of Christ, explaining its purpose, and delineating the differences between an authentic church and some of the nasty caricatures, which are really not church at all. I explained to him that not everything that calls itself "church" really is an authentic church. We discussed how the very nature of what the church is means that it will always attract the hurting, those looking for a place to lord themselves over others, and those who are misdirected. However, there will also be those people who are experiencing growth, healing and transformation in their lives and who consequently begin to manifest an increasing likeness to Jesus and his gathered people, the church.

In the midst of this entire dialogue about the church with my angry and hurting friend, I felt a deep sense that this path—in spite of its hardships—is the one that Jesus calls us to participation in: His authentic church.

Why write another book about the church, when countless others have done so before? I have chosen to do so for a couple of reasons: I wanted to engage in a cathartic process that would strengthen my confidence about the local church and its value both personally and theologically. In addition, I hoped to produce a book that could be used to encourage deeper exploration of the local church by those who are new to faith and those who are disillusioned by their experience with the church.

After many years of stumbling obedience in serving the Lord in His church, I have experienced the good, the bad, and the ugly. It was in this context that I felt the need to consider once again the biblical foundations of the church and challenge and remind myself, if no one else, that the Church is God's idea and therefore to be highly valued.

It has been good and refreshing to think through what scripture says about the church and seek to dream afresh about what the outworking of this marvelous work of God could look like in our own day. It has also been helpful to read the works of others and consider much needed insights on the church. In particular, I have enjoyed the remarkable understandings of Dietrich Bonhoeffer in his little book, *Life Together.* David Watson's insights in *I Believe In The Church* add wonderful color and texture to the topic. There are many contemporary books too numerous to list here which have been useful in this quest.

Over the course of my life, I have also been blessed to encounter some remarkable influences who have deepened my regard for the church and its potential. They include: Rev. Barry Jones (my first pastor), Major Ian Thomas, Dr. Alan Redpath, Rev. Jim Graham, Rev. Charles Price, Rev. Rob Whittaker, Rev. Dr. Bruce Milne, Rev. Timothy Keller, and many, many others.

There are, no doubt, additional vital topics that need addressing with regard to the topic of the church. This book discusses those topics that have been important personal discoveries and which, are foundational for a healthy ecclesiology. My intent has been to write for those who are confused about the importance of the church and for those who are seeking to lead authentic churches in contemporary culture.

Discussion Questions:

1. How would you describe what a church is to someone who had never seen one before?

2. What is the most exciting expression of a church that you have ever encountered?

3. Is there someone you know that has been helpful to you in understanding what church should be like?

Notes

[1] Harvard Magazine, Sept/Oct 2014, . Accessed 9/20/14.
[2] Ibid
[3] Ibid

CHAPTER TWO

Churchless Christianity?

"By faith he went to live in the land of promise, as in a foreign land, living in tents... For he was looking forward to the city that has foundations whose designer and builder is God" (Heb. 11:9-10).

"No offense, but I have seen enough of it all...I'm into Jesus but I don't need the Church." As we sipped a robust dark roast coffee with the gentle beat of a nondescript indie tune playing in the background, our conversation had turned to what I did for work. I said I led a local church and asked Kevin if he had a faith journey in his background. His response revealed some obvious layers of emotion, and I began to gently probe to see if a door to that conversation was likely to open. Sadly, Kevin's comment is one that has become all too familiar in our current culture.

"Forget the Church and Follow Jesus!" This was the cover of a recent Newsweek magazine.[1] It contained an article by Andrew Sullivan proposing that the way of "saving Christianity" in North America is to jettison the useless, old, tired, angry, and hypocritical structure of the church and just follow Jesus.

One of YouTube's recent viral wonders is a short video called, "Why I Hate Religion, But Love Jesus." It reached 10 million views in less than a week—and at the time of writing, had over 23 million views![2] Its creator, spoken word artist Jefferson Bethe, has clearly struck a chord within our culture and much of what he says needs to be heard.

Bethe writes on his YouTube post, "This poem highlights my journey to discover this truth. Religion either ends in pride or despair. Pride because you make a list and can do it and act better than everyone, or despair because you can't do your own list of rules and feel 'not good enough' for God. With Jesus though you have humble confident joy because He represents you, you don't represent yourself and His sacrifice is perfect putting us in perfect standing with God the Father." A fantastic discovery to be sure, for it recovers the crucial truth of the historic Christian message. Unfortunately, many people equate his video message with a call to abandon the church.

Evidence of this growing shift away from church is observed in an editorial by Timothy George who writes, "The fastest-growing demographic in American religious life, is the 'nones,' [which] includes many young people who are drawn to a churchless Christianity."[34]

In North American culture there has been a massive decline in church attendance in the past few decades. In Canada, for example, a recent publication noted that in the past two decades (1986 – 2008) religious attendance has declined by twenty percent![5]

In fact, based on current trends, one Christian denomination in Canada expects its congregations to look like this within fifteen years:

- fifty-two financially supporting households
- zero new members received
- zero new members in Sunday school
- zero baptisms (all ages)
- zero weddings
- four funerals.[6]

In the U.S. there is little more to be encouraged about when it comes to church attendance. In the first decade of the twenty-first century, church attendance has declined by nearly 10 percent. The average congregation in the U.S. declined in size from 130 to 108, with 25 percent of all congregations now averaging less than fifty attendees per week.[7]

The trends are alarming because they indicate that people (the unacquainted) aren't just staying away from church, but those who were previously involved are actively leaving their churches and not returning. The dramatic exodus has been evident in several studies in the North America and The United Kingdom. In fact a 2011 study in Canada has been provocatively titled, "Hemorrhaging Faith."

The study showed that of 2,049 Canadian young adults (ages 18-34), 70 percent attended church every week as children in the 1990s, yet only 27 percent currently attend at all, and 35 percent no longer identify with Christianity.

One of the perceived solutions to this cultural exodus from the church is to simply forget the church and embrace the invitation to join in with Churchless Christianity. Yet the question needs to be asked: is there really such a thing as

"Churchless Christianity" (like a flightless bird)? Or is this more of a failure to understand Jesus and a willingness to instead embrace the broken values of the twenty-first century culture?

To be sure, there may be compelling reasons to avoid some expressions of the church (some of these will be highlighted in what follows), but this book is a call to persist in the journey with Jesus and His body, the church.

One example that compels us not to give up but to continue on, embracing the experience of the church, is hinted at in these words about an ancient faith hero, Abraham. "By faith he went to live in the land of promise, as in a foreign land, living in tents... For he was looking forward to the city that has foundations whose designer and builder is God" (Heb. 11:9-10).

The eleventh chapter of Hebrews is a record of some remarkable men and women, figures who find a place in God's story of history because of their faithful lives. If *Time, Fortune,* or *Politico* were compiling a list of "must know" people from history, none of these folks would likely make the list, but God says they lived noteworthy lives. The common theme of their lives is that they lived faithfully.

Now just what does it mean to live faithfully? Is it having a big house, small house, wired house, frat house, shared house, or no house? Is faithful living characterized by having much or having nothing, by dressing oddly or by having some wild kind of spiritual experience? The biblical record helps us to see that a "faithful life" has little or nothing to do with any of the characteristics just mentioned. So, what does it mean to be a faithful person, and what does this have to do with finding an authentic C.H.U.R.C.H. (an acronym that will be explained in a later chapter)?

Faith might be defined as "learning to see life from God's perspective and living it with His presence in view or more simply put, *believing God*."[8] The people listed in Hebrews 11 lived or died in a variety of circumstances and yet each one exhibited a learned ability to see life from God's perspective and to live it with His promises in view. Interestingly, Hebrews 11 lists more than a dozen major figures of faithfulness, yet the patriarch Abraham gets more press than all the others.

Here was a person who, in spite of his flaws, would not give up pursuing the discovery of that promised city. No doubt he saw some good green places along the way to set up his own city, but he would not settle for less than God's promised city. Abraham was a person whose life was marked by a vision for something lasting—and yet elusive—a city that had God as its designer and builder. This vision is what kept him from settling down in many tempting but inadequate places in life. This vision kept him looking forward in times of trial or times when he was disappointed by those around him.

As we seek to follow Jesus, we can be encouraged by Abraham's example of persistent obedience. Jesus came to establish a new community—the church—which we are called to be a part of, rather than settle for some man-made oasis of individual and privatized faith.

The words recorded in Hebrews 11:9-10 tell us two key things:

1. When God gives a revelation it may be obscured by many factors, but persistence pays off.

2. Refusal to settle for the immediate will ultimately lead to the reward of the permanent.

God's revelation about the church really begins in the Garden of Eden, where we find glimpses of divine and human community. After the crushing blow of sin entering creation, a view of a new community gradually unfolds. At first, this finds expression in the history of Israel, whose flawed experience is filled with prophetic hopes. Finally, the coming of Christ restores the vision of a new community as He speaks of the coming Kingdom. In Matthew 16, Jesus declares that He will establish a new community—a called out people (*ekklesia*)—and that nothing, not even hell, will withstand this advance. Jesus' earliest followers understood this and throughout the ages His followers have been like Abraham: seeking that city whose "designer and builder is God."

As I was writing part of this book at a local university campus, a sudden downpour made it essential to dash into a nearby faculty lounge to dry off. A very welcoming woman on staff gave me a warm place to sit. We made polite introductions, and she asked me what I was doing on campus. When I told her that I was writing a book about finding an authentic church, she became quite excited and began to tell me of a conversation she had following a recent death in her family. She said, "You know, after the funeral we all sat around and discussed the fact that our culture is missing a place where we can find answers to those spiritual life questions, and we need that."

Interestingly, she mused, "We seem to have a spiritual emptiness in our culture." She went on to say that as a result of their recent discussion, her sister had begun attending a church to explore more about these spiritual issues, adding, "We were all like...wow!?" (I guess her family viewed attending a church as a pretty extreme thing!)

In the chapters that follow, we will attempt to rediscover a fresh vision of what this living community of Christ's people is meant to be. We will explore the early source materials—the biblical record—for definitions and observations of an authentic church.

Can you really "follow Jesus and forget about the church" as the Newsweek article advocates? We will see that the church is in fact, the central outcome of Jesus' mission on earth; Christians cannot just ignore it. Jesus did not come to offer disconnected individuals some sort of personal celestial fire insurance so that they could continue living their lives as usual. Instead, Jesus came to rescue them from the weight and tyranny of their sin; and from the rule of the enemy of all good—Satan. The result of that rescue effort is to incorporate people into a new community on earth in which renewed relationships to God, self and others become a possibility.

Jesus came to heal the broken-hearted, and include those healed people in a new society, in His world, which is the church. Ultimately, His plan for the church will culminate in the restoration of a New Heaven and a New Earth, which has given the people of God hope throughout history. We will see that the mission of Jesus' church has much for life now before that final glorious family gathering.

"I have come home at last! This is my real country! I belong here. This is the land I have been looking for all my life, though I never knew it till now...Come further up, come further in!"

– The Last Battle, C.S. Lewis

Discussion Questions

1.   How might you respond to the statement – "I have a private faith and don't see any need for church"?

2.   Do you feel that the church is a place where your secular friends can safely explore their questions about spirituality? Why or why not? What would need to change for that to be a possibility?

3.   What is one insight from this chapter that you find helpful, doubtful, or hopeful?

4.   What are some of the difficult questions you or your friends have about the church?

Notes

[1] April 2012.

[2] http://www.youtube.com/watch?v=1IAhDGYlpqY

[3] Timothy George, Beeson Divinity School.
http://www.christianitytoday.com/ct/2012/june/churchless-jesus.html

[4] Timothy George on Churchless Christianity – "This phenomenon is nothing new. In 1832, Ralph Waldo Emerson, the godfather of privatized religion in America, resigned from his church in Boston and moved to Concord, Massachusetts, to write essays on nature, reason, and self-reliance. Even earlier, in the age of the Reformation, spiritualists such as Sebastian Franck taught that the true visible church had ceased to exist in the world. Thus they no longer baptized, or shared Communion, or preached the audible Word of God. Instead, they focused on the inner light. Every man's hat became his own church... the Protestant reformers took a different approach. They protested with vigor against corruption and abuse in the church, which they aimed to reform but not abandon. They advocated a strong ecclesiology in the service of the Word of God. Calvin went so far as to claim, with Cyprian in the early church, that "outside the church there is no salvation."

[5] "Changing Patterns of Attendance at Religious Services in Canada", 1986–2008 - David E. Eagle. Journal for the Scientific study of Religion. March 2011.

[6] United Church of Canada - http://canadianchristianity.com/study-predicts-united-church-decline-continue-696/

[7] The Hartford Institute for Religion Research released the study's findings Saturday in a report titled "A Decade of Change in American Congregations, 2000 – 2010" authored by David A. Roozen.

[8] Definition given by Dr. Lloyd Jones – in "Believing God", R.T. Kendal.

CHAPTER THREE

Why Bother With Church?

"Jesus, undeterred, went right ahead and gave his charge: 'God authorized and commanded me to commission you: Go out and train everyone you meet, far and near, in this way of life, marking them by baptism in the threefold name: Father, Son, and Holy Spirit. Then instruct them in the practice of all I have commanded you. I'll be with you as you do this, day after day after day, right up to the end of the age'" (Matt. 28:18-20, The Message).

Being an active part of a local church doesn't make you a Christian, but not being a part of one should at least cause you to question whether or not you truly are!

If You Build It They Won't Come

The explosion of "Churchless Christianity" may well be the unpaid debts of neglect in our generation. On one hand, the expression of the church that confronts many people is unattractive and quite unlike the church seen in scripture. Rather than a vibrant gathering of those questing together to follow their Lord at all costs, they find a slick offering of programs, professionals, and events organized in the name of Jesus.

I recently sat in a church worship service that boasted an incredible production with a choir, singers, an orchestra, overhead cameras, large screen projections, and a twenty-eight minute message. After being ushered out so the following service could flood in, I was left wondering whether this experience of "church" would be recognized as such by our persecuted brothers and sisters in Christ in other parts of the world? Would the early Christians even recognize this event as church? It was interesting to see a significant absence of many under the age of fifty in this gathering of some 3000 people.

On the other hand, a truncated gospel message might be contributing to the ambiguity about the value of the church. In efforts to simplify the message of Jesus, we have too often left out the concept that the new life that Jesus gives to us is meant to be lived out in His community: the Church.

A church leader told me about a sensational evangelism program that his church was doing—a topic that genuinely excites me. He described how they had made contacts in the community with hundreds of individuals and shared the gospel with them. They saw dozens and dozens of positive responses to the invitation to follow Jesus! When I asked how they had been able to accommodate all the new Christians, he explained that none had actually begun attending their church. This seemed disappointing to him, but acceptable. Sadly, that sort of outcome is all too common among Christians and underlines what should be a major concern to us. It should alarm us and cause us to ask, "What's wrong?" I suggest that what is wrong is that we have ignored a significant part of the message and mission of Jesus.

The final instructions Jesus gave to His followers, known as the "the great commission" actually make it clear that gathering with others into faith communities is what He has in mind. The point of *training, baptizing, and teaching* is really to form new communities or "colonies of heaven" here on earth. Early Christians were familiar with colonies of Rome in their midst; these were gatherings of citizens who enjoyed many of the benefits of Rome while still living in different localities. The church is a gathering of those living in a different realm—a broken and rebellious world—as we wait for a final triumph of our King.

This is a Football

Coach Vince Lombardi was the legendary coach of the Green Bay Packers from 1959-1967 (he won Coach of the Year in 1959). He racked up ninety-six wins to thirty-four losses, six Division championships, two conference championships, and two Super Bowl wins. Coach Lombardi began his annual training camp speeches with these words: "Gentlemen, this is a football!" He was not making a joke; he was reminding these seasoned athletes, whose lives were given to the game, that if they hoped to become a winning force, they had to know the foundations.

The foundation is where the great coach would begin each season.

If we hope to live in the fullest experience of Jesus' gift of new life, we too need to be clear on the fundamentals. Perhaps too much is assumed in the life of the average church; many of its members do not have a clear idea about what the church is or why God is so excited about it. Sadly, as already noted, some of our teaching and preaching about Jesus' message fails to clearly express that coming to Christ leads to becoming a part of His body, the church.

We can almost hear a "spring training" message for early Christians from another coach, the Apostle Peter:

"As you come to him, a living stone rejected by men but in the sight of God chosen and precious, you yourselves like living stones are being built up as a spiritual house, to be a holy priesthood, to offer spiritual sacrifices acceptable to God through Jesus Christ" (1 Peter 2:4-5).

Notice Peter says here that our coming to Jesus is connected to becoming part of a "spiritual house." Those who received new life through Jesus were not left on their own to privately hold their faith and to personally live out their lives. They were expected to become a part of God's new spiritual community, which is the church.

> "As Christ is precious to the Father, so are we made precious."

The scholar Ed Clowney highlights this truth in his comments on Peter's teaching: "Peter now spells out the wonder of God's salvation: the delight that the Father has in his Son is given to us. As Christ is precious to the Father, so are we made precious." That is the wonderful good news that captures our hearts in the gospel: God loves me, as much as He does His own Son! This news does not leave us struggling on our own as we await heaven; it leads us to find that we are made part of a new family—the church. Clowney continues, "As Christ is the cornerstone of God's temple, so are we stones in that house of God. He is the living Stone; we, too, are living stones." Again, "Peter's language is corporate. He thinks of the spiritual temple, not as the body of an individual believer, but as the body of believers, the company of those who are joined to Christ."[1]

As Peter speaks about being a spiritual house, his listeners would have been thinking of past encounters with God that took place in another spiritual house, the Jewish tabernacle, and later the temple. Their history was one of God revealing Himself and transforming lives in that specific place.

The Church in God's Plan

If you were God and wanted to show all of creation your wisdom, what plan might you choose? The Apostle Paul tells us that God's plan to accomplish this is through the Church! Christians embrace the Church of Jesus Christ because it is central to God's plan and because it is where God can be encountered. God says that it is through the church that His wisdom will be shown to all of creation!

"To me, though I am the very least of all the saints, this grace was given, to preach to the Gentiles the unsearchable riches of Christ, and to bring to light for everyone what is the plan of the mystery hidden for ages in God who created all things, so that through the church the manifold wisdom of God might now be made known to the rulers and authorities in the heavenly places. This was according to the eternal purpose that he has realized in Christ Jesus our Lord" (Ephesians 3:9-11).

As Christians we are not called to sort this out for God. He does not need reminding that there is some pretty spotty history with the Church. Once we see that this is the means through which He has chosen to reveal eternal mysteries, our concern should be how we can be a part of an authentic expression of what the church is meant to be.

Communion Sanctorum

The early Christians clarified many of the core truths of the Christian message that were held in common by followers of Christ using creedal statements. One of those early statements of faith, the Apostles' Creed, likely dates in part to the second century. It was vital that creeds like this were recited, as the majority of the early church was illiterate. One of the statements recited therein is, "I believe in the Holy Ghost; the holy catholic Church; the communion of saints; the forgiveness of sins; the resurrection of the body; and the life everlasting. Amen." The Church, in its larger (universal) and local (communion of the saints) expressions, is affirmed as a core part of God's mission in the world as stated in the creed.

The late Whitehouse hatchet man turned Christian statesman, Charles Colson, wrote a summary of Christian beliefs in his book, *The Faith*. He clarifies that a central part of God's mission in our world is to form believers into a community of saints.

> As individual Christians, we are also called to be part of a specific confessing body, or local church...

"On the cross, Christ not only reconciles us to Himself but incorporates us into His body, the Church, which consists of all those who have accepted Christ's offer of salvation—what the early Church called the communion sanctorum, the community of the saints. As individual Christians, we are also called to be part of a specific confessing body, or local church, where our spiritual duties and disciplines can be fulfilled."[2]

Putting it Together

So *what* is the church?

First we need to remember *what the church is NOT.* The Church is not: a building, a religious organization, a social club, a political movement, or a denomination. Then, what is a church? It can be helpful to consider the word "church" as an acrostic to attempt to give a memorable way to grasp the richer breadth of what the church is when we see it in the Bible.

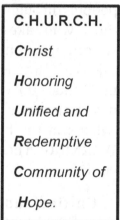

C.H.U.R.C.H.

Christ

Honoring

Unified and

Redemptive

Community of

Hope.

C.H.U.R.C.H. = a Christ Honoring, Unified and Redemptive, Community of Hope. This acrostic is a shorthand text for the fuller picture given to us of the early church, as found in the book of Acts, chapter two.

"And they devoted themselves to the apostles' teaching and the fellowship, to the breaking of bread and the prayers. And awe came upon every soul, and many wonders and signs were being done through the apostles. And all who believed were together and had all things in common. And they were selling their possessions and belongings and distributing the proceeds to all, as any had need. And day by day, attending the temple together and breaking bread in their homes, they received their food with glad and generous hearts, praising God and having favor with all the people. And the Lord added to their number day by day those who were being saved" (Acts 2:42–47).

Christ Honoring

Honoring Jesus Christ is foundational to the formation of the church. That may seem overly obvious, but the demise of many movements of the church throughout history has always begun when the foundation of their life together is anything else. Christ honoring is seen in the desire to hear and understand His Word, obey His voice, and give Him worship (Acts 2:42-43). The true church has always been focused on the person of Jesus Christ. His work on our behalf is to be celebrated; this is what gives us a certain hope of forgiveness and new life. His voice is sought in the reading, teaching and preaching of His Word. This teaching and preaching is not just to inform us about Bible facts but also, to hear from the Lord Himself who continues to speak to His people through His word. Authentic church is found among those who take seriously the Word of God as living, active, and supreme in all matters of life. A couple of important questions to ask are: "How is this key issue of Christ Honoring seen among us?" and, "Do we seek Him together and seek to discern His direction, or is our only guiding principle more likely to be 'what's in the budget?' or 'what's been our traditional habit?'" WARNING: These are signs of serious spiritual decay in the church.

Unified and Redemptive

Once again looking at the Acts 2 passage we read, "And all who believed were together and had all things in common...." When Jesus prayed for His followers prior to giving His life on the cross, He asks the Father for unity in His church.

"I am praying for them. I am not praying for the world but for those whom you have given me, for they are yours... Holy Father, keep them in your name, which you have given me, that they may be one, even as we are one" (John 17:9-11).

Unified means to be in unity, which is not the cookie-cutter image of looking similar, living in the same suburbs, even being of the same age and stage in life. To be genuinely unified is a God-inspired gift that has incredible power in the world. It is so precious that we can be assured if there is no unity a church will cease to exist.

"Their unity will itself be a victory over the devil, since part of his strategy will be to attack it. It will also be part of their armory against him, since their fellowship will be an expression of the *power of* God's *name*, which protects them. This unity will be patterned after the unity of the Father and Son (11). It is therefore a vastly richer reality than social camaraderie."[3]

A.W. Tozer once said the best way to keep 100 pianos in tune, is not trying to tune each one to the others, but by tuning each to the perfect pitch of a tuning fork. In the same way best way to experience unity in the church is to encourage each one to pursue and humble and obedient walk with Christ and unity will be a byproduct.

Redemptive does not mean that any group of Christians can redeem a person; only the work of Jesus makes that possible. Titus 3:5 says "He saved us, not because of works done by us in righteousness, but according to His own mercy, by the washing of regeneration and renewal of the Holy Spirit."

To redeem means to "buy back" and this is what Jesus has done for us on the cross. Because we are confident that the

> To be a redemptive community is not just a new slogan.

work of Jesus is sufficient to save anyone, we gladly join Him in making that news of His rescue known to as many people as possible.

Being a "redemptive community" has been described like this: "It is the call to take broken, wounded individuals and in the presence of Christ's love, grace, salvation and healing transform them into a powerful force for the kingdom of God."[4]

To be a redemptive community is not just a new slogan—it requires a major move away from our selfishness and a choice to follow Jesus into truth, transparency, and trust. The truth in God's Word, with its piercing clarity and transparency, is about our own brokenness and need for a savior. We choose to trust Jesus that together with only the meager resources of our own, we have access to His limitless resources for our lost and broken world. We join Him in promoting the liberating message that anyone can enter into the joy of redemption.

The Apostle John encourages us in this direction of living as a redemptive community by using the imagery of living together in light not wandering in the world's darkness. "But if we walk in the light, as he is in the light, we have fellowship with one another, and the blood of Jesus His Son cleanses us from all sin." (1 John 1:7). He is telling us that the way to experience genuine spiritual freedom in our lives is found in intentional transparency around the Cross. "Christians who live in God's light do not find it difficult to walk together in fellowship. The light shows the way ahead, and enables them to co-ordinate their actions and move forward in harmony. Where Christians are at variance, or separate from one another, it is always true that someone is already walking out of fellowship with Christ. This does not mean that we shall all agree about everything, but that is not the essence of fellowship anyway. It is about loving one another and valuing one another, so that we can agree to differ without severing the ties that bind us to one another as sons and daughters of the light."[5]

Community of Hope

An authentic church must be more than a sixty or ninety minute church service a few times each month; it is a call to live life together. The twentieth century martyr, Dietrich Bonhoeffer, wrote a wonderful book on the nature of the church called *Life Together*. At great personal cost, he led an example of what this community could look like, even in the face of oppression and death. Bonhoeffer encouraged his students to live in the light and humility of Christ with each other, and not allow pretense to separate them. He is clear that this type of community is only possible because of a common life in Christ.

"Our community with one another consists solely in what Christ has done to both of us. This is true not merely at the beginning, as though in the course of time something else were to be added to our community; it remains so for all the future and to all eternity. I have community with others and I shall continue to have it only through Jesus Christ. The more genuine and the deeper our community becomes, the more will everything else between us recede, the more clearly and purely will Jesus Christ and his work become the one and only thing that is vital between us. We have one another only through Christ, but through Christ we do have one another, wholly, and for all eternity."[6]

Once again, in Acts 2, we see this aspect of church displayed in the words: "And they were selling their possessions and belongings and distributing the proceeds to all, as any had need. And day by day, attending the temple together and breaking bread in their homes, they received their food with glad and generous hearts...."

This is not some Marxist utopianism or wealth redistribution enforced by an authority structure. This is a Spirit-filled liberty that releases people from their bondage to the idols of culture. This generosity is the expression of doing life together and embracing the needs of one another in sacrifice. The result of worshipping, celebrating, and doing life together is community. When this is seen it will inevitably make an impact on our lonely planet.

> This is a Spirit-filled liberty that releases people from their bondage to the idols of culture.

When I want a picture of what the community of hope can do, I think about a dear friend, Emmanuel. As a young boy growing up in Ghana, West Africa, Emmanuel was orphaned and left with few dismal hopes for life. Eventually he lived with distant relatives and several other children in a simple rural structure without power or water. It was in those years that he was told of God's love and the care that he could experience through Jesus. This news was welcoming to him, and he soon found a new family—God's spiritual house, the church. This new community helped him to overcome many obstacles and gave him many opportunities to grow as a young man. Emmanuel and I became friends as he came to complete his PhD in North America. He will return as a leader in his nation and his church. Though he calls me his pastor, I have found so much I need to learn from him when we are together, brothers in community, the church.

Corpus Christi

Jesus is God the Son who came into our world and was confined to a finite human body like ours. He was chosen to do this so that He might offer Himself as a perfect sacrifice for the sins of all of humanity and thereby offer liberty to a race enslaved. He also offered His creation a clear view of their creator for the first time.[7] After His triumph over sin, Satan, and death, Jesus prepared for the next phase of His work on our behalf, a work that takes place in Heaven itself. However, His work on earth is not done; it just switches bodies! His presence on earth continues in a new body, made up of people from every background and culture. These people are those who, having understood what a marvellous sacrifice Jesus made for them, have received His forgiveness and been infused with a new quality of life. They have chosen to walk together with Jesus in a different direction and at a new pace, loving and obeying Him above all else. This new direction and lifestyle sets them apart from the rest of the world around them. It is a costly life, but the rewards are much greater.

Our bodies are a vehicle to express our essence in time and space. Without a body you could not be known in this realm of time and space in which we live. Your uniqueness—unseen and within—can be witnessed in the ways you behave and the actions you choose. This new "Corpus Christi" (body of Christ) is the means by which God's presence can be seen and known in the world. Before Jesus came into the world, there were faint glimpses of God to be had, but Jesus comes as the greatest "*ikon*" in whom God can be known.

> This new "Corpus Christi" ... is the means by which God's presence can be seen and known in the world.

The church is now Christ's body on earth. God's intention is that His essence might be seen in the actions of this new group of people. It should be said, "When you look at the church then you can see what Jesus is like." Wow! That can be pretty hard to reconcile if you have been around the church much! Yet since God is committed to the Church being His 'Corpus Christi' on earth, we can be sure He will provide the resources needed to achieve that end.

The comparison between the Church and the body of Christ is made for us in 1 Corinthians 12:12-27:

"For just as the body is one and has many members, and all the members of the body, though many, are one body, so it is with Christ. For in one Spirit we were all baptized into one body—Jews or Greeks, slaves or free—and all were made to drink of one Spirit. For the body does not consist of one member but of many. If the foot should say, 'Because I am not a hand, I do not belong to the body,' that would not make it any less a part of the body. And if the ear should say, 'Because I am not an eye, I do not belong to the body,' that would not make it any less a part of the body. If the whole body were an eye, where would be the sense of hearing? If the whole body were an ear, where would be the sense of smell? But as it is, God arranged the members in the body, each one of them, as he chose. If all were a single member, where would the body be? As it is, there are many parts, yet one body.

"The eye cannot say to the hand, 'I have no need of you,' nor again the head to the feet, 'I have no need of you.' On the contrary, the parts of the body that seem to be weaker are indispensable, and on those parts of the body that we think less honorable we bestow the greater honor, and our un-presentable parts are treated with greater modesty, which our more presentable parts do not require. But God has so composed the body, giving greater honor to the part that lacked it, that there may be no division in the body, but that the members may have the same care for one another... Now you are the body of Christ and individually members of it."

6 Truths about the Body of Christ from 1 Corinthians 12

1. The church *is called* the body of Christ (vs.27); it does not say the church is like a body, or is best pictured by a body, but it *is* the body of Christ. If the mission of God in our world is going to be completed then we can be sure that it will be done through the Church. How wonderful that we are, by God's grace, made a part of it.

2. Every member must participate if the body is going to be effective (vs. 14). When anyone does not participate, the body will be less able to present the ministry of Christ in the world. To put it another way, it takes the whole body of Christ to complete the whole work of Christ. If we choose to remove ourselves from the fellowship of the body, we will suffer and the body will suffer consequently. The failure in some churches today is that few members have a place in which to participate.

3. There is no room for inferiority about our place in the body of Christ. All members matter in the body, but not all have the same place or function (vs. 15-16). The eye, the foot, the ear, and countless other body parts—each is a wonderful part of our body and plays a special role. Thank God for intercessors, administrators, encouragers, teachers, givers, etc. each finding their place in the body of Christ so that it can complete the work of Christ in the world.

4. All of us need to know our limits (vs. 17-18). God has arranged the body as He sees fit, and He does not intend that every person attempt every activity. Just as a healthy

body has defined parts and roles, so we will serve best in the particular places God has gifted us.

5. We need to affirm others in their God-given roles (vs. 20-21). Much feedback we receive in life seems to be negative; the church could be the one place where that is different. How wonderful it is to hear words of affirmation and encouragement about God's gifting and design in our lives. Others in the body will discern and grow, as they are lovingly encouraged in areas of gifting.

6. We need to value unity highly (vs. 24-25). God gives greater honor to some parts of the body as He sees fit. Our focus must be on His gracious and underserved call to include us in His body while asking Him to help us to value unity more than our personal ambitions.

You are Invited...But Don't Bring Your Spouse!

Can you imagine getting an invitation to an event with that sort of message? It would be easy enough to turn that one down because the toxic message conveys that what is precious to you has been rejected by the sender. The bride of Christ is another image in the Bible used for the Church. God sees the Church in a way that is remarkable. When we say no to the church then we are telling Jesus that what He finds most wonderful, we want no part of. We are to "bother" with church because it takes the central part of God's plan in history and because it is the body of Christ, where we can join Him in His mission in our world.

Discussion Questions

1. What is one point from this chapter that makes you most uncomfortable?

2. Do you think the acrostic C.H.U.R.C.H. is helpful? Why or why not?

3. Look again at the passage from 1 Corinthians 12. What does it say to our view of other churches?

4. Is Churchless Christianity a valid way to pursue following Jesus in our world?

Notes

[1] E. P. Clowney, *The Message of 1 Peter: The Way of the Cross* (Leicester, England; Downers Grove, IL: InterVarsity Press, 1988), 87-88.

[2] Chuck Colson, *The Faith*, Zondervan 2008. Page 147.

[3] Bruce Milne, *The Message of John: Here is Your King!* (Leicester, England; Downers Grove, IL: InterVarsity Press, 1993), 245.

[4] Jay Haug
http://www.virtueonline.org/portal/modules/news/article.php?storyid=13826#.UL0m6oWmDww

[5] David Jackman, *The Message of John's Letters: Living in the Love of God*, The Bible Speaks Today (Leicester, England; Downer's Grove, IL: InterVarsity Press, 1988), 30–31.

[6] Dietrich Bonhoeffer, *Life Together: The Classic Exploration of Christian Community* (HarperOne,1978).

[7] Hebrews 1:1-3

CHAPTER FOUR

Plugged In God's Power for the Church

"But you will receive power when the Holy Spirit comes on you; and you will be my witnesses in Jerusalem, and in all Judea and Samaria, and to the ends of the earth" (Acts 1:8).

The story is told of Thomas Aquinas,[1] a former noble and a remarkable theologian who had embraced a life of simplicity. He was invited to Rome and was given a tour of the splendor of the city and the Vatican. After being shown around the vast complex of wealth his guide mused "No longer need we say, silver and gold have I none!" To which Aquinas replied, "That is true, but neither can we say, in the name of Jesus Christ, rise up and walk!"

An authentic church is a gathering of people who have discovered God's gift of power for a life that is inexplicable, except in terms of God. The church is not just another club or society that has an honorable purpose or goals to meet. Too often, what we see in the name of the church is a powerless or fractured organization that has stuff, but no authority to overcome what Satan has ruined in life. We have even developed ways of acting and believing that excuse our inability to say "Rise up and walk." Those are the humble and yet confident words of those who know that God's great power is accessible for the daily challenges of life. This power for life is nothing less than the presence of God's Spirit within His people. The sad reality is that, to paraphrase A. W. Tozer, in many church scenarios, if God were to totally remove the presence of the Holy Spirit, few would notice any difference!

A generation ago, Englishman J. B. Phillips translated the Bible into contemporary language for his day. He relates that the experience of this project gave him new insight into God's power and purpose in the church. He wrote the following in the preface of his translation of the Book of Acts:

"It is impossible to spend several months in close study of the remarkable short book, conventionally known as the Acts of the Apostles, without being profoundly stirred and to be honest, disturbed. The reader is stirred because he is seeing Christianity, the real thing, in action for the first time in human history. The new-born Church, as vulnerable as any human child, having neither money and influence nor power in the ordinary sense, is setting forth joyfully and courageously to win the pagan world for God through Christ.

"Yet we cannot help feeling disturbed as well as moved, for this surely is the Church as it was meant to be. It is vigorous and flexible, for these are the days before it ever became fat and short of breath through prosperity, or muscle-bound by over-organization.... They did not make acts of faith—they believed; they did not hold conferences on psychosomatic medicine, they simply healed the sick... They did not say their prayers—they prayed... But if they were uncomplicated by modern standards, we have ruefully to admit they were open on the God-ward side in a way that today is almost unknown..."2

Just imagine what it would be like to be living in a new experience of power—God's power to defeat temptation—to live as a forgiving person, to pray with a new authority, and to know deeper joy. Imagine what being in a group of others who are experiencing these same realities might be like. How would life be different?

One of my hobbies is road biking. Recently I was riding with a group along the seaside in severe winds of up to 70 mph (100 kph). The wind was so strong that it took considerable effort to move forward and to avoid being blown off our bikes. Our outbound ride was a battle the whole way, but then we changed direction and began our ride home. As I began to climb the last big hill before home, I suddenly realized that I was being pushed by the great power of the wind and almost effortlessly reached the top. I thought, "This is a great picture of the filling of the Holy Spirit." We battle along in our strength, making little progress until we yield to His empowering, and then things change.

Some Reasons for Our Lack of Power

While this is not an exhaustive list, these three reasons certainly cover much of the ground for our weakness regarding the Holy Spirit. For a long time in the church the person and work of the Holy Spirit has been *ignored, misunderstood,* and *resisted.*

The Holy Spirit *Ignored*

"And he said to them, 'Did you receive the Holy Spirit when you believed?' And they said, 'No, we have not even heard that there is a Holy Spirit'" (Acts 19:2).

In Acts 19 we have the record of some people who are seeking to follow Jesus, but who quite obviously are missing out on the promised power of God's presence. While this passage may have some controversial interpretations, it must be seen at the very least as a warning not to settle for impotent inspirational principles; God's plan is for His people to be living testimonies of a new supernatural power.

There is a clear and present danger today of simply reducing the Christian life to principles and formulas. It is often an implicit message that all one needs is to believe right truths about Jesus, practice some select spiritual disciplines and the outcome will be fruitful lives. This ignores the essential reality of the person of the Holy Spirit and His ministry among us. Listen to the words of A. W. Tozer on this ignorance of the Holy Spirit:

"The Doctrine of the Spirit as it relates to the believer has over the last half century been shrouded in a mist such as lies upon a mountain in stormy weather. A world of confusion has surrounded this truth. The children of God have been taught contrary doctrines from the same texts, warned, threatened and intimidated until they instinctively recoil from every mention of the Bible teaching concerning the Holy Spirit. This confusion has not come by accident. An enemy has done this. Satan knows that Spiritless evangelicalism is as deadly as Modernism or heresy, and he has done everything in his power to prevent us from enjoying our true Christian heritage."[3]

> "The Doctrine of the Spirit has... been shrouded in a mist such as lies upon a mountain in stormy weather."

The Holy Spirit *Misunderstood*

The highway of spiritual experience is littered with the wreckage of those who have misunderstood the person and work of the Holy Spirit. On one hand, the Holy Spirit is not to be feared as one who will carry us into outrageous behaviors (which sadly some have been taught to expect). On the other hand, the Holy Spirit is not a personal genie to be controlled for selfish purposes or ecstatic experiences.

At the end of the Gospel of Matthew, Jesus commissions His disciples to make more disciples, baptizing them "...in the name of the Father and of the Son and of the Holy Spirit..." (Matt. 28:19).

Authentic Christians affirm that, rightly understood, the Holy Spirit is no less than an equal member of the Trinity. The Holy Spirit is not a force or power, but a person of the Godhead who is both precious and all-powerful, just as Jesus and the Father are. The Holy Spirit is the personal and powerful presence of God in the life of a Christian. He has all the characteristics of personhood. He speaks (Acts 1:16), thinks (Acts 15:28), leads (Rom. 8:14), can be grieved (Eph. 4:30), and can be resisted (Eph. 4:30).

The Holy Spirit *Resisted*

Despite the clear biblical teaching of who the Holy Spirit is and what He does in the life of the Church, His presence is often resisted. Why would that be? Ultimately, because Satan is effective in deceiving Christians about their true inheritance from the Father.

"In him [Jesus] you also, when you heard the word of truth, the gospel of your salvation, and believed in him, were sealed with the promised Holy Spirit, who is the guarantee of our inheritance until we acquire possession of it, to the praise of his glory" (Eph. 1:13-14).

Additionally, the Holy Spirit is resisted because of our power struggles—He wants complete control! Even after believers have let Him into their lives, they won't take full advantage of relinquishing control by allowing Him to permeate their lives.

When a pilot is being trained to recover his aircraft from a stall, the instructor must teach the pilot to release control and let the natural design of the aircraft take over. If the pilot will not let the correction take place and insists on wrestling the controls, the outcome is disastrous. So too, when the church or individual Christian wrestles for control, the result is disastrous.

God's Spirit has been given to us to bring power and passion for Jesus. In Acts chapter 1, the promise of God is fulfilled at Pentecost—the Holy Spirit is poured out. This was not something that was hidden from onlookers; there was an obvious change in the lives of those who had been filled with the Holy Spirit. It wasn't like there was a sudden onslaught of "niceness" or great social justice projects that had the town in an uproar; rather, an awareness that these people were fully alive. The onlookers couldn't make sense of what had happened to them.

The Filling of the Holy Spirit

In Ephesians we are shown the difference between the old life that is characterized by darkness and fruitless lives, and the new life that God's spirit brings when we are filled with Him.

"For at one time you were darkness, but now you are light in the Lord. Walk as children of light (for the fruit of light is found in all that is good and right and true), and try to discern what is pleasing to the Lord. Take no part in the unfruitful works of

darkness, but instead expose them. For it is shameful even to speak of the things that they do in secret.

But when the light exposes anything, it becomes visible, for anything that becomes visible is light. Therefore it says,

> *'Awake, O sleeper,*
> *And arise from the dead,*
> *And Christ will shine on you.'*

"Look carefully then how you walk, not as unwise but as wise, **making** *the best use of the time, because the days are evil. Therefore do not be foolish, but understand what the will of the Lord is. And do not get drunk with wine, for that is debauchery, but be filled with the Spirit, addressing one another in psalms and hymns and spiritual songs, singing and making melody to the Lord with your heart, giving thanks always and for everything to God the Father in the name of our Lord Jesus Christ, submitting to one another out of reverence for Christ"* (Eph. 5:8-21).

God's directive here for all Christians is to be filled with the Holy Spirit (verse 18). In order to better understand this vital power for life together, let us consider the following three questions:

- WHAT does it mean to be filled with the Holy Spirit?

- WHY do we need to be filled with the Holy Spirit?

- HOW can we be filled with the Holy Spirit?

What does it mean to be filled with the Holy Spirit?

John is a dear friend and mentor of mine, and for many years he was an upstanding church member and successful lawyer. He relates how he had a deep hunger within for a greater love for

God and experience of His presence. In spite of knowing the words of creeds and liturgies, he did not know a transforming experience of God in his life. One night he and his wife were invited to a service where they understood for the first time the wonderful work of the Holy Spirit, and there began a whole new journey. It was like the difference between a beautiful picture of a feast and actually being at the feast to enjoy it. The transforming work of the Holy Spirit led John to a life of fruitful ministry, which included pastoring a leading church in his city. Now in his 80's John continues to have a meaningful influence in the lives of many people and offers them spiritual wisdom and practical advice. Over the past few years he has lovingly cared for his wife until her death. The image of

> All Christians are indwelled by the Holy Spirit (Romans 8:9), but not all are filled by the Holy Spirit (Ephesians 5:18).

All Christians are indwelled by the Holy Spirit (Rom. 8:9), but, not all are filled by the Holy Spirit (Eph. 5:18). Interestingly, in Acts 6 when servers were needed in the church, the believers were told to "Choose seven men from among you who are known to be full of the Spirit and wisdom." If all Christians were "filled," the believers would not have needed to be told this was something to look for.

Being filled with the Holy Spirit is more than attending a great service, but the ongoing condition of their lives. These were Monday to Saturday worshippers! It is nice when someone comes and enters into worship songs, but an authentic church needs people living in the Lord's presence. However—then as now—it is possible to be filled with various things as a Christian, but God wants it to be His Holy Spirit who fills, controls, and guides us. To be filled with the Holy Spirit means that the Holy Spirit *is* the One who dominates our personality and determines our behavior. Rather than battle over some of the terminology on this matter, we need to clarify the question whether this is my experience and if not, why not? The great pastor D. Martyn Lloyd-Jones says it this way:

"So the way to test whether we are filled with the Spirit is to ask: Are we full of thankfulness? Are we full of praise? Do we sing to ourselves and to one another in psalms and hymns and spiritual songs? Do we make melody in our hearts? Do we praise God when we are alone? Do we delight in praising Him with others? Do we delight in praising Him in public as well as in private? Are we full of the spirit of praise, of thanksgiving, of worship and adoration? It is an inevitable consequence of being filled with the Spirit. This is something that can happen many times. The baptism, I suggest, is the initial experience, the filling is an experience that can often be repeated."[4]

Why Do we Need to be Filled with the Holy Spirit?

A simple answer could be that scripture tells us to be—and why would we settle for less? In addition, we need to be reminded that this is God's gift to restore us to normal living—the presence of the Creator in His creature. Interestingly, the first explanation given about the crowd on the Day of Pentecost stated, "These men have had too much wine. They are drunk" (Acts 2:13). In fact, that explanation was so prevalent that when Peter got up to preach, the first thing he said in verse 14 was, "These men are not drunk, as you suppose. It's only nine o'clock in the morning." The pub is not even open yet; it's not that! The Apostle Paul tells us, "Do not get drunk on wine, which leads to debauchery. Instead, be filled with the Spirit" (Eph. 5:18). He makes a

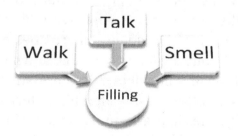

connection similar to that which the people at the Pentecost event made; the issue is, what *controls* us?

Think about it, how do you get drunk? You submit your being under the control and power of something else. There are three general signs, which identify someone who is drunk: their walk, talk, and smell. Maybe this is why Paul contrasts drunkenness with Spirit-filling, because being filled with the Holy Spirit also affects our walk, talk, and smell.[5]

WALK – this is the term in the Bible for how we live our lives. Galatians 5:16 says, "Walk in the Spirit." That means as you go through life, it is the Spirit who is determining how you live and behave. Ephesians 5:2 says, "Walk in love," for it is the Holy Spirit who is the Spirit of love. As you walk through life full of the Spirit, there are certain aspects that characterize you which can only be explained by the indwelling Spirit of Christ. Rather than following our old pathways and stumbling in our decisions, relationships, and choices, the Holy Spirit will empower us to live in ways that please God.

TALK – being filled by the Holy Spirit will affect the way we talk. Jesus gave a very accurate barometer of the human heart when He said, "Out of the abundance of the heart the mouth speaks" (Matt. 12:34). If you want to know what is taking place in someone's heart, listen to what comes out of his or her mouth. In other words, whatever fills our hearts is what we will talk about. When you are with a group of Christians, where does the conversation go? Is there talk about the latest episodes of what's hot on TV or who got voted off of some show? Is there strong speech about political parties and the latest leadership failure or is there fresh joy about God's blessing and the wonder of the gospel? What are our conversations filled with?

Notice in the passage above—"...but be filled with the Spirit, addressing one another in psalms and hymns and spiritual songs" (Eph. 5:18-19)—there is a change in what comes out of the mouth. On the Day of Pentecost, being filled with the Spirit, they all spoke in other tongues as the Spirit enabled them. When Paul said, "Be filled with the Spirit," his next words were, "Speak to one another, sing and make music in your heart to God." Praising God in song is an integral part of worship because being full of the Spirit gives us something to sing about!

SMELL – in 2 Corinthians 2:14-15, Paul writes, "Thanks be to God who always leads us in triumphal procession in Christ and through us spreads everywhere the fragrance of the knowledge of Him. For we are to God the aroma of Christ among those who are being saved and those who are perishing. To the one, we are the smell of death; to the other, the fragrance of life."

Recently, I was reunited with a college friend in London whom I had not seen in many years. We had a wonderful evening, enjoying some great Asian food, and talking of the many twists and turns of life. When we were driving home, I said to my wife, "Wow those folks were such a breath of fresh air! What was it that made that visit so refreshing?" It was the aroma of Jesus coming through the whole conversation, and this seemed to give us great new strength.

The atmosphere of our lives points to Christ. To some, it is the smell of life that draws them, while to others it is the smell of death. That is why when you live in the fullness of the Holy Spirit, people are either going to oppose you or gravitate to you.

How to be filled with the Holy Spirit

We had a gas fireplace in a previous home; much of the time it looked like a dark cavity with a tiny glimmer of light at the back. With the flick of a switch, you could enjoy the full power that was there waiting for combustion. Some Christians and churches seem to have only the "pilot light" of the Holy Spirit on in their lives and need to have the switch thrown. While this is something only God can do in our lives, are there any actions we can take to give Him room to throw the switch?

Lighting the Fire

There are no human formulas to the Spirit's fullness, but these are some actions that will certainly help.

1. Eagerly and entirely surrender yourself to Him— by faith in His blood we are cleansed from all guilt and shame (1 John 1:9). Many of us will fight this experience of filling, wondering, "What will I lose? Will I lose all my plans, hopes, and desires?" Often these are Satan's whispers of protest—resist him! Don't just choose passive acquiescence, but actively choose full cooperation with the Spirit.

2. Confess any known sin or rebellion. Tell Him you don't want to grieve Him any longer, nor resist Him. You want Him to flood all areas of your life and give you a deeper love for Jesus. The story of Achan in Joshua 7 is a picture of hidden sin and the resulting consequences. There can be no fullness of the Spirit if we are attempting to hide sins from God.

3. Invite the Holy Spirit to fill you afresh, empower you, and make you a witness of Jesus. Express to Him your deep desire and desperate need for His control.

4. Eagerly Pursue Him. Jesus Himself assures us that He only wants good for us, and we don't need to be afraid in the area of the empowerment and filling by the Holy Spirit; these words are recorded by both Matthew and Luke and are the words of Jesus so we can trust him!

"So I say to you: Ask and it will be given to you; seek and you will find; knock and the door will be opened to you. For everyone who asks receives; the one who seeks finds; and to the one who knocks, the door will be opened.

"Which of you fathers, if your son asks for a fish, will give him a snake instead? Or if he asks for an egg, will give him a scorpion? If you then, though you are evil, know how to give good gifts to your children, how much more will your Father in heaven give the Holy Spirit to those who ask him!" (Matt. 7:9-11).

The Scottish theologian Rev. A. B. Bruce, in his classic work on discipleship, challenges readers to wholeheartedly pursue wholeheartedly the fullness of the Holy Spirit:

"To such as do not desire the Holy Spirit above all things, Jesus has nothing to say. He does not encourage them to hope that they shall receive any thing of the Lord; least of all, the righteousness of the kingdom, personal sanctification. He regards the prayers of a double-minded man, who has two chief ends in view, as a hollow mockery—mere words, which never reach Heaven's ear."[6]

Is Power the Goal?

If we finished this chapter at this point it could be misleading and incomplete, it would have left out a vital aspect of the Holy Spirit's filling in our lives and His church – the experience of His Joy! This is much more than happiness or excitement, which occurs when our circumstances are good: a happy marriage, a good job, or healthy kids. In fact, *joy* is much less tenuous than feelings of happiness; it is the deep contentment of our soul that results from being filled with our Maker's delight and pleasure. All people long for this joy and pursue it in myriads of ways, which consistently fail, but Jesus spoke of it as an outcome of the Holy Spirit's work.

After I had been following Jesus for a few years and training for ministry, I was made aware of the joyful reality of the filling of the Holy Spirit in my life. A learned and godly pastor explained to me the role of the Holy Spirit, for me as his follower, and for His church. He explained the greater power, love and joy that was possible to be known in the Spirit's fullness. Up to that point I had been an eager believer in Jesus and yet longed for more intimacy and joy in following Jesus. That experience, and many subsequent ones, produced a profound sense of joy and delight in the Lord that has remained in spite of incidents, which crushed my happiness, but they could not take the joy of the Lord.

The writer of Psalm 63 reflected on this:

"1 You, God, are my God, earnestly I seek you;
I thirst for you, my whole being longs for you,
in a dry and parched land where there is no water.

2 I have seen you in the sanctuary and beheld your power and your glory.
3 Because your love is better than life, my lips will glorify you.
4 I will praise you as long as I live, and in your name I will lift up my hands.
5 I will be fully satisfied as with the richest of foods; with singing lips my mouth will praise you."7

The Psalmist's longing for the Lord's fullness and for the joy the Lord can give is described like a despairing person in the desert and craving a drink. (vs.1) This is an apt image of the human condition, thirsting for more, but not finding satisfaction at the many mirages of our world. Then, an encounter with the living God in which His true greatness is seen changes everything for the writer. (vs.2) The experience of His love is real and transforming and seems to be a greater discovery than anything else in life, and what flows from that encounter is joy, great and immense joy! (vs.3) The result is a new language of praise and prayer that overflow from a full heart, a joy that comes from a new source.

Jesus speaks about this source of joy that comes to our souls through being satisfied in God's presence. For example, in John 4 he meets a woman whose soul thirst was expressed in a series of broken relationships. Jesus tells her that she was drawing from a well that was inadequate for her thirst, but that she could be satisfied by the results of His coming.

"Jesus answered, 'everyone who drinks this water will be thirsty again, but whoever drinks the water I give them will never thirst. Indeed, the water I give them will become in them a spring of water welling up to eternal life.'"[8]

Later in John 7 we learn that this living water in a person's life is the result of the filling of the Holy Spirit and it is a picture of that satisfying and joyful experience of his indwelling.

[38] Whoever believes in me, as Scripture has said, rivers of living water will flow from within them." [[39] By this he meant the Spirit, whom those who believed in him were later to receive. Up to that time the Spirit had not been given, since Jesus had not yet been glorified."[9]

Not only is there joy for the Spirit-filled Christian, but the effect of that joy is a powerful attraction to Jesus in the watching world. In fact, the lack of the joy in those who profess to know

Him may be what keeps many people from looking more closely at Jesus and His Church. As Dr. Martyn Lloyd Jones in his book *Spiritual Depression* wrote, "Unhappy Christians are, to say the least, a poor recommendation for the Christian Faith; and there can be little doubt but that the exuberant joy of the early Christians was one of the most potent factors in the spread of Christianity."[10]

We are offered so much in the gift of the Holy Spirit. The place we should long to live is in His fullness, so that His abounding joy is ours, in spite of all our circumstances. It is a reminder to us to desire and eagerly expect the joy of the Lord as we allow the Holy Spirit to fill us afresh.

A. W. Tozer said: "I must agree with the psalmist that the joy of the Lord is the strength of His people. I do believe that the sad world is attracted to spiritual sunshine—the genuine thing...When the warmth and joy of the Holy Spirit are in a congregation...and the folks are spontaneously joyful, the result is a wonderful influence upon others...I have said it a hundred times: The reason we have to search for so many things to cheer us up is the fact that we are not really joyful and contentedly happy within.... But we are Christians, and Christians have every right to be the happiest people in the world!"[11]

The power and presence of the Holy Spirit filling each of us, as Christians will both enable and endear the witness of Christ in His people in the world. This does not mean a blissful unhindered life of happiness, but joy in whatever circumstances life in this world brings.

Discussion Questions:

1. What is there in our lives together that is evidence of the power of God's Spirit at work in us?

2. Imagine being in a group of others who are experiencing the Spirit's fullness. Discuss how that might be different from where things are now.

3. Rather than battle over some of the terminology on this matter, we need to clarify the question "Is this my experience?" and if not, why not?

4. What topics are our conversations filled with?

5. Read the Ephesians 5 passage again, what are a few of the insights that you see there?

6. Write out a prayer inviting the Holy Spirit to fill you afresh. Include some of the details found in this chapter. Take time to be alone with Him and wait on Him in prayer.

7. What has been your experience with experiencing "Joy in the Lord" as the outcome of being filled with the Holy Spirit? How can we encourage each other in this area?

Notes

[1] Aquinas (A.D. 1225 – 7 March 1274) was born into nobility in Naples in the thirteen century. His conversion to Christ led him to renounce his power and wealth to serve God. He is one of history's great theologians and one of the major influences of Western thought.

[2] J. B. Phillips, translator, *The Young Church in Action,* (London: G. Bles, 1955).

[3] Essay: How To Be Filled With The Holy Spirit - A. W. Tozer - http://www.sermonindex.net/modules/newbb/viewtopic.php?topic_id=226 32&forum=34&4

[4] D. M. Lloyd-Jones, *God the Holy Spirit,* (Wheaton, IL: Crossways Books, 1997), 242-243.

[5] I am indebted to Charles Price of People's Church Toronto for this analogy.

[6] A. B. Bruce, *The Training of the Twelve; or, Passages out of the Gospels, Exhibiting the Twelve Disciples of Jesus under Discipline for the Apostleship* (Oak Harbor, WA: Logos Research Systems, Inc., 1995), 60-61.

[7] Psalm 63:1-5, NIV

[8] John 4:13,14 NIV

[9] John 7:38,39 NIV

[10] Lloyd-Jones, David Martyn. Spiritual Depression: Its Causes and Cure. Grand Rapids, MI: Wm. B. Eerdmans, 1965. Print.

[11] A. W. Tozer, *Tragedy in the Church: The Missing Gifts, 10-*

CHAPTER FIVE

Keeping the Main Thing the Main Thing

"You crazy Galatians! Did someone put a hex on you? Have you taken leave of your senses? Something crazy has happened, for it's obvious that you no longer have the crucified Jesus in clear focus in your lives. His sacrifice on the cross was certainly set before you clearly enough. Let me put this question to you: How did your new life begin? Was it by working your heads off to please God? Or was it by responding to God's Message to you? Are you going to continue this craziness? For only crazy people would think they could complete by their own efforts what was begun by God"
(Galatians 3:1-3 The Message).

Mid-life hit Mitch hard, and he was lost as to what it was that gave his life a purpose; thus, his search for meaning began in earnest. That is the plot line in the movie *City-Slickers* starring Billy Crystal as Mitch and Jack Parlance as a wizened old cowboy named Curly. Mitch has a busy life full of all the usual pursuits, but he finds himself increasingly confused, disappointed and empty. His journey of self-discovery takes him on an adventure at a western dude ranch. While learning about the workings of a cattle ranch, Mitch meets an old cowboy name

Curly who seems to be quite contented and might be able to answer his question about the meaning of life. A classic dialogue ensues:

> *Curly: Do you know what the secret of life is?...*
> *Mitch: No, what?*
> *Curly: This. [he holds up one finger]*
> *Mitch: Your finger?*
> *Curly: One thing. Just one thing. You stick to that and everything else don't mean [anything].*
> *Mitch: That's great. But what's the "one thing"?*
> *Curly: [smiles] That's what you gotta figure out.*

Many Christians and church leaders need to discover afresh what the "one thing" is for the church. They have found themselves in a flurry of church activities and following pursuits that have begun to fade in their attraction. The question that arises is, are we doing the main thing that Jesus calls us and commissions us to? Leaders and committed Christians need to ask a few questions: what is really important in the life of the church and in our investment of life together? Are we possibly stuck in a malaise or routine that is familiar but lacking a compelling sense of purpose? What is the one thing or the main thing for the church, and is that what will restore vibrancy to our lives as Christ's community in the world?

There have been many and varied answers given to the question of what the main thing is over the ages. Answers such as spiritual gifts, worship music styles, ecclesiastical organization, versions of the Bible, gender roles, and so it goes. All of these are valuable, but they are not the main thing. The ongoing challenge in the life of an authentic church is to keep the main thing, the main thing. When we move away from that position everything else moves off course.

This is the point of Paul's words in Galatians 3, which Eugene Peterson translates so graphically in his Bible paraphrase, The Message. The Apostle Paul is at pains to startle this community of believers into returning to the main thing. "You crazy Galatians! Did someone put a hex on you?" He says it was like a spell had been cast over them and had caused them to wander off down some dark dead-end trail, rather than walking on the bright path of light that is found in Jesus alone. The theological sidetrack for the church at Galatia was the idea that certain behaviors were needed to earn a right standing before God. Jesus' finished work for them was not enough, and they needed additional actions to please God. *"How did your new life begin? Was it by working your heads off to please God? Or was it by responding to God's Message to you?"* They had begun to make other things the main thing. They were majoring on the minors, and minoring on the majors; this was certain to lead to spiritual oblivion.

Discussion about the main thing, or the priorities of the Church has been held *ad infinitum*, in the history of the church. However, the guiding principles for the discussion must come from the words of Jesus, the head of the church.[1] His final words have been called the Great Commission,[2] and in them, we are told that His people are to continue His work of reaching lost people in the world. John Stott reminds the church of its priorities, "In the Church's mission of sacrificial service, evangelism is primary." In other words, many things are valuable in the Church's engagement within society, but we must not lose sight of the paramount need to share the good news of God's rescue mission through Jesus Christ.

In Matthew's version of the Great Commission, Jesus tells us that His presence will be with those who are engaged in His mission of reaching lost people, "Go into the world and make disciples...and *behold I am with you* always." He says that if the

Church stays focused on this as the main thing, they will know a great sense of His personal presence. Certainly, the thing that is most satisfying in the life of a church is the manifest presence of Jesus.

It is important to clarify that this work of evangelism is not in contrast to discipleship; the two are inseparably linked. You cannot be a disciple if you are not following your Master, seeking and saving the lost. However, when lost people come to Christ, it is crucial that they learn how the character of Christ is formed in them, for that is discipleship. Unfortunately, at times, evangelism has been reduced to reciting a few correct beliefs, with no expected life-change. At the same time, discipleship has been reduced to learning Bible facts and doctrines.

Thankfully, these two vital concepts of evangelism and discipleship have been re-united and re-empowered with the recovery of the understanding of biblical "mission." The church has been reminded that its call is to be first and foremost "missional"–a term coined by the missionary scholar Leslie Newbigin.[3] He has reminded the church that all Christians are called to live as missionaries in whatever culture they are in. This will mean being intentional about sharing the good news of Christ with those around them, and being intentional about growing in likeness to Christ Jesus.

The Main Thing is Mission

For many churches today, the topic of mission and promoting the gospel is at best ambiguous. In fact, a variety of positions on this priority for the church are evident simply by observation of its activities. Look at the calendar and budget of a local church, and it will become fairly clear where its priorities lie. The positions taken regarding promoting the gospel may include the following:

- Confusion about the content of the gospel, a "therapeutic moralistic deism."[4]

- Passivity about promoting the gospel because of living in a pluralistic culture.

- Rejection of the need for the gospel, rooted in a "soft universalism."

- Active and intentional engagement for the gospel.

The accompanying diagram (Diagram 1) can help a church reflect on where it finds itself and consider the need for a course correction.

New Testament scholar Michael Green has contrasted the clear priority on evangelism or mission in the early church and the priorities of contemporary church in this way:

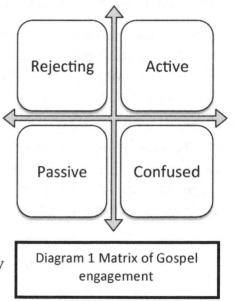

Diagram 1 Matrix of Gospel engagement

"The early church made evangelism its number one priority. Today it comes far down the list. Many local churches have, I suspect, never once debated it in their decision making body.

The early church had deep compassion for people without Christ. Many sections of the modern church are far from convinced that it matters whether you know Christ or not. Other religions are nearly, if not quite as good. Humanists live blameless lives, and in any case, God is far too loving to damn anyone.

The early church was very flexible in the ways it preached the good news, but utterly opposed to syncretism of any sort. Many churches today are rigid in their preaching methods, but thoroughly open to syncretism.

The early church was sensitive to the leading of the Holy Spirit. In modern churches of the West, managerial skills, committee meetings and endless discussions generally replace serious dependence on the guidance of God.

The early church was not unduly minister-conscious. There is a notorious difficulty in attempting to derive definitely any modern ministerial patterns from the New Testament records. Yet, today, everything hinges on the minister. The paid servant of the church is expected to engage in God-talk, others are not.

The early church expected every member to be a witness to Christ and His risen presence and power. Today witness is at a discount compared with dialogue; and it is only expected of certain gifted clergy at best, and not run-of-the-mill lay people.

In the early church buildings were unimportant: they did not own any during the period of the churches greatest advance. Today buildings seem all important. Their upkeep consumes the money and the interest of the members, often plunges them into debt, and insulates them from those who do not go to church. The very word 'church' has changed its meaning. It no longer denotes a company of people: it means a building.

In the early church, evangelism was the spontaneous, natural chattering of good news. It was engaged in continuously, by all types of Christians, as a matter of course and privilege. Today, it is a spasmodic, highly organized, expensive and usually dependent on the skills and the enthusiasm of visiting specialists.

In the early church, the policy was to go out where people were and make disciples of them. Today it is to invite people along to churches where they feel ill at ease, and subjects them to sermons. Today's church attempts suction, invitation, in-drag. The early church practiced explosion, invasion, outreach.

In the early church, the gospel was frequently argued about in the philosophical schools, discussed in the streets, talked over in the laundry. Today it is not discussed very much at all, and especially not on secular ground. It belongs in church on a Sunday, and a properly ordained minister should do all the talking.

In the early church, whole communities seem to have come over to faith together. In the atomized church of the West, individualism runs riot, and evangelism like much else, tends to reach its climax in one-to-one encounter.

In the early church, the maximum impact was made by the changed lives and quality of community among the Christians. Today much Christian lifestyle is almost indistinguishable from that of those who profess no Christian faith, and much church fellowship is conspicuous for its coolness.

It is worth reflecting on these remarkable contrasts, along with the no less striking contrasts in the effectiveness between the early church and ourselves. If we want to take evangelism seriously in the local church, we could do no worse than go back to our roots."[5]

Luke 10 - The Jesus Pattern for Missional Ministry:

The ongoing pattern of church history seems to be one of discovering and recovering old truths over and again, then seeing them revitalize us by the power of the Holy Spirit. This is the challenge that Michel Green stated in his final phrase above: "If we want to take evangelism seriously in the local church, we could do no worse than go back to our roots." Recently, I have been seeking to do that more seriously by studying and applying the words of Jesus in His commissioning of the earliest disciples. His words are found in Luke 10 where we find Jesus sending out a larger group of disciples to share in His mission. While these words were specific to that original group, they seem to have timeless principles that can send us into a fresh new experience of dynamic mission.

Those who came to follow Jesus and to learn from Him were then sent out ahead of Him, to introduce Him to others. The seventy were to go "into every town and place where he himself was about to go."[6] Look at the words of Luke 10:1-20:

"After this the Lord appointed seventy-two others and sent them on ahead of him, two by two, into every town and place where he himself was about to go. And he said to them, "The harvest is plentiful, but the laborers are few. Therefore, pray earnestly to the Lord of the harvest to send out laborers into his harvest. Go your way; behold, I am sending you out as lambs in the midst of wolves. Carry no moneybag, no knapsack, no sandals, and greet no one on the road. Whatever house you enter, first say, 'Peace be to this house!' And if a son of peace is there, your peace will rest upon him. But if not, it will return to you. And remain in the same house, eating and drinking what they provide, for the laborer deserves his wages. Do not go from house to house. Whenever you enter a town and they receive

you, eat what is set before you. Heal the sick in it and say to them, 'The kingdom of God has come near to you.' But whenever you enter a town and they do not receive you, go into its streets and say, 'Even the dust of your town that clings to our feet we wipe off against you. Nevertheless know this, that the kingdom of God has come near.' I tell you, it will be more bearable on that day for Sodom than for that town.

"Woe to you, Chorazin! Woe to you, Bethsaida! For if the mighty works done in you had been done in Tyre and Sidon, they would have repented long ago, sitting in sackcloth and ashes. But it will be more bearable in the judgment for Tyre and Sidon than for you. And you, Capernaum, will you be exalted to heaven? You shall be brought down to Hades.

"The one who hears you hears me, and the one who rejects you rejects me, and the one who rejects me rejects him who sent me.

"The seventy-two returned with joy, saying, 'Lord, even the demons are subject to us in your name!' And he said to them, 'I saw Satan fall like lightning from heaven. Behold, I have given you authority to tread on serpents and scorpions, and over all the power of the enemy, and nothing shall hurt you. Nevertheless, do not rejoice in this, that the spirits are subject to you, but rejoice that your names are written in heaven.'"

Insight to Equip and Encourage Us in Mission

The words of Jesus found here in Luke 10 should encourage us with these insights:

- "The Harvest *IS* plentiful..." not was, nor will be, nor is somewhere else, but IS now, right where we are. This is what Jesus sees and says to encourage us to move out with Him. We see barriers, rejection, and hardness of hearts; He sees a harvest ready to reap.

- God is already at work in people around us; we can join Him. We don't have to create hunger in others; we can take it by faith in His word that God is already working in people all around us.

- Our task is to discern where He is working by going and sowing and watching. There is no pressure on us to make something happen; He will guide us to good soil.

- Jesus Himself will come when we obey; we can expect to meet Him in new places. Luke tells us these were places that Jesus was about to go, and we will find Him there if we go out.

Among the many things that we can learn from this passage, it seems clear to me that there is a simple model for the church that chooses to engage with Jesus in mission in His world. That simple model is a three-part strategy for evangelistic mission that we might call *Prayer, Care, & Share*. What follows is an expansion and explanation of each of these parts.

A. PRAYER: Luke 10:1-2

"The harvest is plentiful, but the laborers are few. Therefore pray earnestly to the Lord of the harvest" (Luke 10:2).

Principle: Spiritual Breakthrough Will Begin With Prayer.

Jesus says, "The harvest is plentiful, but the laborers are few, therefore...." Now, if we had to write out the next part of His statement, we might put a variety of words next such as, therefore, recruit others... Therefore, form a committee... Therefore, raise funds... Therefore, get going... Therefore, start an awareness campaign... But Jesus says, "Therefore, PRAY." That is the solution that Jesus offers for a great harvest to be reaped. If we are going to see lost people won to Christ and our hearts inclined toward them, there is only one solution—prayer.

A renowned pastor of the nineteenth century, A. T. Pierson, once said, "There has never been a spiritual awakening in any country or locality that did not begin in united prayer." Other great leaders of past eras, such as Andrew Murray or Jonathan Edwards, echo the same message: in united and persistent prayer will come breakthrough.

The Revival Historian Dr. J. Edwin Orr researched and chronicled this reality of prayer in many parts of the world and varied times in church history. His study and subsequent writing demonstrated that the most unlikely gatherings for prayer led to the most substantial experience of spiritual awakenings that changed whole societies. From the great awakenings in the United States in the eighteenth and nineteenth centuries to the Welsh Revivals of the early twentieth century, all were rooted in united prayer.[7]

What to Pray For:

The teaching of Jesus in this passage suggests several things that we are to pray for. At various times, our focus in prayer - may need to be with greater attention to one or another in the following areas. These areas of prayer can be both personal and corporate.

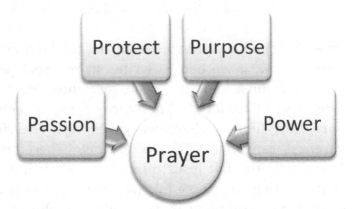

➤ PASSION – We are to ask the Lord to give us His heart for the harvest. This area of our praying for passion can include:

    I.   Laborers – we are to pray for more of them for His harvest, which is so great. *"Lord, send more!"* Warren Wiersbe says, "Instead of praying for an easier job, they were to pray for more laborers to join them, and we today need to pray that same prayer. (Please note that it is *laborers*, not spectators, who pray for more laborers! Too many Christians are praying for somebody else to do a job they are unwilling to do themselves.)"[8]

    II.   Also prayer for more of His heart for the harvest! *"Lord, send me!"* Our prayer to God for His harvest will have the effect of changing our hearts and causing us to feel more of His heart for lost people.

➤ POWER – We need to pray for the power of the Holy Spirit if we are going to see a harvest. This is not something we can do in our strength or wisdom. Notice again verse 17: "The seventy-two returned with joy, saying, "Lord, even the demons are subject to us in your name!" They saw spiritual breakthrough–not just good presentations, but God setting people free. We can ask God for the power of His Holy Spirit to fill and flood us so that He can do mighty works through our obedience.

➢ PROTECTION – "I am sending you out as lambs in the midst of wolves" (Luke 10:3). Jesus' words warn us that there is conflict and danger in mission and therefore our prayers must include praying together for spiritual protection.

A. W. Tozer reminds us of the reality of spiritual warfare when he writes, "Show me an individual or a congregation committed to spiritual progress with the Lord, interested in what the Bible teaches about spiritual maturity and victory, and I will show you where there is strong and immediate defiance by the devil!"[9]

Spiritual warfare is learning to pray strategically in the authority that is given to us as members of God's family. We often think that this is only happening elsewhere, but the reality is that we are blinded to this area by our failure to engage in mission and evangelism. A recent message by the great Sri Lankan Christian leader Dr. Adjith Fernando admitted to having a lack of spiritual warfare in his own ministry, because his activities posed little threat to the spiritual enemy. He said, "We had no spiritual attack in our ministry because we never practiced evangelism!" In other words, there was no threat to the kingdom of darkness; and as a result, no experience of conflict. However, Fernando said when they re-focused on the mission of God and in particular evangelism, they had to learn to stand against spiritual conflict.[10]

➢ PURPOSE – "Carry no moneybag, no knapsack, no sandals, and greet no one on the road (Luke 10:4). In essence, Jesus is encouraging us to travel light as we go in life; to pray, "Lord, don't let us get bogged down with non-essentials." Many things that occupy us in our churches are not evil, they are simply "drags" that slow us down and take us out of a missional lifestyle.

A leader of a previous generation, R. A. Torrey, gives guidance on how to pray with regards to being a church on mission in our world: "Pray definitely for a spiritual awakening, pray that the members of the church be brought onto a higher plane of Christian living, that the church be purged from its present compromise with the world, that the members of the church be clothed upon with power from on high and filled with a passion for the salvation of the lost. We should pray that through the church and its membership, many may be converted and that there be a genuine awakening in the church and community. Any church or community that is willing to pay the price can have a true revival. That price is not building a tabernacle and calling some widely-known evangelist and putting large sums of money into advertising and following other modern methods."[11] That price, insists Jesus, is to pray which has been the discovery of revival movements throughout church history.

B. CARE: Luke 10:3-6

"When you enter a home, greet the family, 'Peace.' If your greeting is received, then it's a good place to stay. But if it's not received, take it back and get out. Don't impose yourself" (Luke 10:5-6 MSG).

Principle: Relational Engagement is required for Mission

Jesus' instructions to His disciples about mission in Luke 10 continue by stating that prayer must be the foundation. When prayer has become our priority and practice, there is another step to take: caring for those we encounter. His instruction to go and enter homes may be both literal and metaphorical; it means to cross-relational thresholds. Hospitality is one of the greatest ways to show that we care for others. This is most often shown by entering either our home with others, or us entering theirs. Entering a home shows that we value and care for those around us. The principle is to demonstrate *care* for those for whom we are praying. We see that this is what Jesus has done for us. John 1:14 tells us He has moved into our world to show His love. His example in His earthly ministry is often of entering a home and caring for those He meets. Remember Zacchaeus (Luke 19:1-10)? Jesus said to him, "Hurry and come down, for I must stay at your house today" (vs. 5). Later we read that salvation came to his household because Jesus took time to care for him.

Caring Involves Going!

"Go your way; behold, I am sending you out..." (Luke 10:3).

Too much of the contemporary church's mission is based on "attraction." Indeed the church should be attractive, with worship that engages even the curious who don't yet know Christ personally. However, the command of Jesus is to *go out* into society, to look for those who are interested and receptive and when invited, to enter their homes. Wow! Think of the evangelistic impact of Christians opening their homes and entering the homes of others. This is not a home invasion, but a willingness to enter the places of comfort of those around us or to invite them into our lives.

As our world urbanizes, one of its desperate needs is community: belonging and caring. All around us are lonely people, students from other nations, families who have been transferred, singles due to death or divorce, and refugees driven from their nations. Caring for people, taking an interest, and showing love in a practical way is vital. If we would be intentional and choose to invite them into our homes, we might find that, like Zacchaeus, salvation comes to them.

Care and Spiritual Probes

"Whatever house you enter, first say, 'Peace be to this house!'" (Luke 10:5).

Principle: Look for places where God is at work, i.e. where the harvest is ready.

As we build relationships with those around us, it is quite useful to test the ground with the use of what I call *spiritual probes* to discover what God has been doing in their lives and whether there is more openness. Consider using some of these:

Spiritual Probes: the purpose in probing is to explore spiritual readiness and to listen. As we try to discern *is God at work here and now in this person,* we are not simply trying to download our prepared answers into their minds! These types of probes can be very useful in gauging where someone is at spiritually.

Examples

1. Invite probe: Invite those you care for to something, which might deepen their spiritual insight.

> "82% of those invited to church will go if invited by a trusted friend!"

"I would love to have you as my guest next week at church/event, and go for coffee after! Would that work for you?"

Author Thomas Rainer in his book, *The Unchurched Next Door*, notes his research shows that 82 percent of people invited to church will go if a trusted friend invites them! That should greatly encourage our hearts to invest in prayer and care.

2. Belief probe: Using disarming questions can be helpful in spiritually significant conversations. Here are a couple of examples:

    a. Do you think God cares for you personally?

    b. What are your spiritual beliefs?

    c. What do you think about Jesus?

    d. If that weren't the whole story, would you want to know what I've found?

3. Personal Probe: being willing to offer up some of our personal story in a non-threatening way can be very useful, when done in a way that offers safety to our friend.

"If you ever wanted to hear how Jesus has changed my life—I would love to tell you."

4. Prayer probe: offering to pray for or even with our friends in times of challenge is a wonderful way to approach personal faith in Christ Jesus. This can be offered in a gracious way that is rarely refused.

"I find prayer important—is there anything that I could pray for you this week?"

I have had people say to me after a simple prayer for their healing or troubles, "*Wow! No one has ever prayed for me before....*" At times just the act of praying will touch them and may open doors. How much more when God does a wonder in their life? A young man who was invited to a home group we held received prayer and the next week reported a wonderful experience that made him hungry to know more about Christ. Sometimes praying with the person will not be at the right time or won't be an action they are comfortable with, but we can assure them we care and will continue to remember them in our prayers.

Jesus calls us to care for others, and that may be in a personal way as we pray, visit or encourage someone close to us. However, as an authentic church, that caring may also be expressed as we learn to care for the community around us. We need to pray and discern about what God sees in our area and ask Him for wise ways to express His care in there.

An example of caring for others in a community in Jesus' name is a small group of Anglican Christians in my area of Victoria, Canada. After enduring a difficult and painful situation, this group found themselves without their traditional building and comforts, gathering in a school in a very different neighborhood. The new area was a great contrast to what most of them were used to. Instead of peaceful suburbs, nice yards, and economic stability, they found broken homes, gang violence, drug trades, and desperation. Rather than fleeing to safety elsewhere, they began to pray for the area and ask God how they could be a part of sharing the good news of Christ in this new locality. They felt the answer was to begin demonstrating the love of Christ through caring for the area. Many single parent homes were in need of practical and emotional support. A small food-bank has now been established in the community center that helps dozens of homes every week. A children's day camp was run during the school break to assist families who had no other options for children's activities. Now a Sunday dinner is served in a dignified manner, giving families a chance to go out and have a family experience. The Sunday dinner includes an optional time of singing and discussion of some of Jesus' stories. This act of caring is leading to an ongoing opportunity of sharing.

C. SHARE: Luke 10:8-12

"Heal anyone who is sick, and tell them, 'God's kingdom is right on your doorstep!'" (Luke 10:9 MSG)

The action of evangelistic mission begins with *prayer*, moves onward in demonstrating *care* for those around us, and should culminate in the chance to *share* the reason for our hope. The expectation of Jesus for His followers, as seen in His words here in Luke 10, is that they will share His good news in the places where they are welcomed. The prayer and caring are crucial, but there is another step needed in order for people to understand what it is that compels Jesus' followers. We need to speak up about the Good News, which shows how it is now possible to live under God's rule because of Jesus' finished work. The tyranny of self-rule, sin's rule and Satan's rule has been broken through the cross of Christ. There are many around us who are desperate to hear this from the lips of Jesus' people.

"Here is a challenge; and many might feel that while 'following' is within their capabilities, 'heralding' (sharing) is only for those who are specially gifted. But the passage contains more than one hint that every Christian is expected to do both."
12

What Message did the Earliest Christians share with others?

The New Testament opens its account with "the gospels," which are so called because the early church recognized them as the record of its foundational message. These records were the good news they had come to believe and proclaim. Mark describes the life of Jesus with this term, "The beginning of the gospel of Jesus Christ..." (Mark 1:1). Matthew states that the gospel (*euangelion*) is what Jesus taught and proclaimed, "And he went throughout all Galilee, teaching in their synagogues and proclaiming the gospel of the kingdom and healing every disease and every affliction among the people" (Matt. 4:23). Clearly, the gospel was the message of the early church and was well known to those who had identified themselves with Jesus.

However, the "good old gospel" that many have heard today may not be either good enough or old enough! The term "gospel" may be so familiar that it has become almost meaningless to many and in need of a review. Likely, there is a need to deconstruct some of the popular concepts of the gospel message to help us see that it is not about notions such as making others like us, getting a pass card for heaven's gates, believing a correct set of Bible truths, or promising to make us healthy and wealthy. As Christopher J. H. Wright comments, "One of the dangers with a word like 'gospel' is that we all love it so much (rightly), and want to share it so passionately (rightly again), that we don't take time to explore its full biblical content."[13]

The content of the gospel message, which spread widely in the ancient world, is the full story of what is recorded in the earliest records of Jesus Christ's life as found in Matthew, Mark, Luke, and John. As John Dickson writes "...authentic 'gospel telling' will always recount the broad narrative of Christ's life, as told in the books we call the Gospels."[14]

While the full story of Jesus was spread as the gospel message, it is also possible to detect a few synopses of the gospel that are found in the New Testament which clarify that core message. One such synopsis, and perhaps the fullest, is found in 1 Corinthians 15:3-5, which scholars agree was a creedal statement that goes back to within two to four years of the cross of Christ![15] As such, it helps to illuminate just what those earliest followers of Jesus understood about Him.

"Now, brothers and sisters, I want to remind you of the gospel I preached to you, which you received and on which you have taken your stand. By this gospel you are saved, if you hold firmly to the word I preached to you. Otherwise, you have believed in vain. For what I received I passed on to you as of first importance: that Christ died for our sins according to the Scriptures, that he was buried, that he was raised on the third day according to the Scriptures, and that he appeared to Cephas, and then to the Twelve. After that, he appeared to more than five hundred of the brothers and sisters at the same time, most of whom are still living, though some have fallen asleep (1 Cor. 15:1-6 NIV).[16]

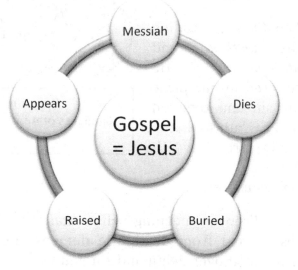

Notice the five points that are given as an outline of the gospel;

1. Jesus' identity as the Christ

2. Jesus' saving death

3. Jesus' burial

4. Jesus' resurrection

5. Jesus' appearance to witnesses[17]

Another way to group this gospel summary of Jesus' life and the message preached about Him would be to say that the apostolic messages highlight His Cradle, Cross, and Crown.

- The Cradle, meaning his *incarnation*. God has humbled Himself and became a human; the Creator entered His creation to rescue and restore it.[18]

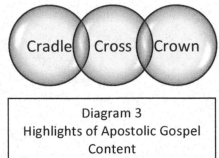

- The Cross-, meaning His *substitution* and *atonement*. He suffered in our place for sin and took on God's wrath so that we might receive His perfect righteousness.[19]

Diagram 3
Highlights of Apostolic Gospel Content

- The Crown, meaning His *exaltation*. He was resurrected from death; He demonstrated that He triumphed over death and sin and will return to rule over a renewed creation.[20]

J. Gresham Machen writes, "The great weapon with which the disciples of Jesus set out to conquer the world was not a mere comprehension of eternal principles; it was a historical message, an account of something that had happened; it was the message, 'He is risen'"[21]

The gospel is the strikingly Good News, set in history, that in Jesus' life, death, and resurrection, God has inaugurated a new chapter in human history. It is about all that God has done on behalf of His creation to bring about a restored future. As Timothy J. Keller says— including something of the human response—"[T]he 'gospel' is the Good News that through Christ, the power of God's kingdom has entered history to renew the whole world. When we believe and rely on Jesus' work and record (rather than ours) for our relationship to God, that kingdom power comes upon us and begins to work through us."[22]

The Gospel is a Powerful and Essential Message

The New Testament conviction about the gospel is that this news has in it the power to transform people who receive and embrace it. In Romans 1:1-4, the Apostle Paul gives another of his synopses of the gospel. A few verses later, he asserts that this message is both powerful and essential for everyone.

"For I am not ashamed of the gospel, because it is the power of God that brings salvation to everyone who believes: first to the Jew, then to the Gentile. For in the gospel the righteousness of God is revealed—a righteousness that is by faith from first to last, just as it is written: 'The righteous will live by faith'" (Rom. 1:16-17 NIV).

The gospel is *explosive,*" (*dunamis*) says Paul; its power is both personal and universal. Personal: people experience the gospel personally, and they can expect transformation. For example, he reminds the church at Colossae that they had been freed from their former destructive lifestyles: "In these you too once walked, when you were living in them" (Col. 3:7). This was the result of the power of the gospel in them.

The gospel is also *universal* in that it is for "everyone who believes" (Romans 1:16).

It is inclusive in that it is for everyone, yet exclusive in the sense that Jesus must be responded to by each individual. This unique message then needed to be taken far and wide so that everyone would have the opportunity to believe in Him. As N. T. Wright writes, "The whole Christian gospel could be summed up in this point: that when the living God looks at us, at every baptized and believing Christian, he says to us what he said to Jesus on [the day of his baptism, 'you are my beloved son in whom I am well pleased']. He sees us, not as we are in ourselves, but as we are in Jesus Christ."[23] The power of the gospel is strong enough to change the condition and position of each and every person who surrenders to Him and believes.

The New Testament contains several snapshots of early Christian messages that were shared with those who would hear them.[24] Scholars have studied these messages and sought to distill the common threads that seemed to be spoken consistently in the various contexts. The technical term for the common core of these messages is the word *kerygma*. It is the Greek term used for preaching or proclaiming in the Bible, and it denotes the irreducible essence of Christian apostolic preaching.

"'It pleased God,' says Paul, 'by the foolishness of the Preaching to save them that believe.' The word here translated 'preaching,' kerygma, signifies not the action of the preacher, but that which he preaches, his 'message,' as we sometimes say."[25]

Theologian C. H. Dodd famously summarized this ancient Christian kerygma in the New Testament[26] as follows (I have added a key word before each for clarity):

1. Happened - The Age of Fulfillment has dawned, the end times which were foretold by the prophets has come.

2. Him - This has taken place through the birth, life, ministry, death and resurrection of Jesus.

3. Honor - By virtue of the resurrection, Jesus has been exalted at the right hand of God as Messiah and head of the new Israel.

4. Help - The Holy Spirit in the church is the sign of Christ's present power and glory.

5. Hope - The Messianic Age will reach its consummation in the return of Christ.

6. Heed - An appeal is made for repentance with the offer of forgiveness, the Holy Spirit, and salvation.

How is the Gospel Advanced by the Early Church?

What may surprise (and relieve) Christians who desire to "live on mission" with Jesus is that the Apostle Paul's prescription is not "button-holing" people with abrasive presentations, but rather embracing a mission-focused lifestyle. The pattern for that mission lifestyle for the Apostle Paul, which he learned from Jesus, and which he taught early Christians, is seen in 1 Corinthians 10:31-11:1 where he says "So whether you eat or drink or whatever you do, do it all for the glory of God. Do not cause anyone to stumble, whether Jews, Greeks or the church of God—even as I try to please everyone in every way. For I am not seeking my own good but the good of many, so that they may be saved. Follow my example, as I follow the example of Christ."

The mission-focus is guided by the desire to live for the glory of God first, using freedom wisely so that others who watch will be drawn to the Lord. At the same time, avoiding activities that cause people to stumble (turn away) from Christ. (As John Dickson notes, "Throughout Paul's letters 'stumbling' usually refers to missing out on salvation."[27]) Consider the following "constellation of actions" that are a vital part of the church's advance of the gospel.

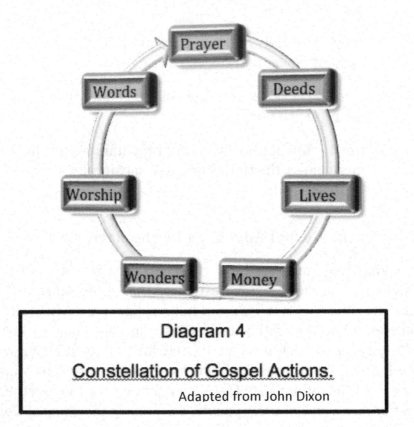

Diagram 4

Constellation of Gospel Actions.

Adapted from John Dixon

Prayer: Paul reminds his partners in the gospel at Philippi that victory was possible through their prayers. A foundational action for the advance of the gospel is the prayer life of the church. (More will be said on this in the final section.)

Deeds: Jesus taught that doing good deeds would be one way that others come to believe in and worship God. (See Matthew 5:16.) Early in the life of the church, there is a noted clear concern for those who were poor and alone.[28] Food banks, micro lending, medical care, practical service, companionship for the lonely -- these and countless other activities have enabled others to give glory to the Father in heaven.

Lives: Jesus made clear that the unity of our lives as His people would be an evidence of His reality.[29] John Stott writes, "...the invisible God, who once made himself visible in Christ, now makes himself visible in Christians, if we love one another. It is a breathtaking claim. The local church cannot evangelize, proclaiming the gospel of love, if it is not itself a community of love."[30]

In addition to purity of love for each other (unity) as a gospel sign, there is also the purity of character (ethics) that points to God's truth. Peter encourages holy living so "...that they may see your good deeds and glorify God..." (1 Pet. 2:12). Again Christopher Wright says, "The Bible...is passionately concerned about what kind of people they are who claim to be the people of God. If our mission is to share good news, we need to be good news people. If we preach a gospel of transformation we need to show some evidence of what transformation looks like."[31]

Money: The church at Philippi was commended for generous giving and support, and affirmed in the means of advancing the gospel. Paul clearly connects giving as a part of mission in Philippians 1:5, when he writes, "because of your partnership in the gospel from the first day until now." As John Dickson affirms, "If we are financially supporting the work of the gospel, we are full partners in this task."[32]

Wonders: Jesus sent out the group of seventy disciples (Luke 10) with the charge to heal and deliver those they met in need and to proclaim His kingdom. As they returned to Him, they reported the amazing experience of seeing the power of God at work. God's people can be confident to pray for all they meet in need and know that He will authenticate His word.

Worship: Peter links worship and mission in 1 Peter 2:9, when he writes, "that you may proclaim the excellencies of him who called you out of darkness into his marvelous light." God's people in the Old and New Testament were called to worship Him among the nations, and this worship would have a missional effect. Worship of God is declaring His character and acts of power; these truths draw people to Him.

Words: Doubtless, the advance of the gospel requires spoken words; works alone are not enough to introduce others to the "word made flesh." From texts such as Acts 8:4 and 11:19ff, it is evident that ordinary Christians were verbal witnesses. While not all Christians have the gift of declaring the gospel, Peter says that all of them need to be ready to defend the reason for their hope (1 Pet. 3:15-16).

The Main Thing...

The secret to vibrant spiritual life in an authentic church is connected to keeping the main thing, the main thing. Jesus modeled the mission of God in His life. He was empowered by the Holy Spirit to fulfill that mission, and He was affirmed by the Father for staying on that task. Jesus' final words to the church are to join Him on mission. His promise is of His presence as His church keeps that calling as paramount, "Go therefore and make disciples of all nations, baptizing them in the name of the Father and of the Son and of the Holy Spirit, teaching them to observe all that I have commanded you. And behold, I *am with you* always, to the end of the age" (Matt. 28:19-20, emphasis mine).

> "When the Lord commands, he enables. And his enabling is his presence."
>
> – Michael Green

In His comments on these final words of Jesus in Matthew, scholar Michael Green says:

"The Gospel that began with the assurance that this baby to be born would be Immanuel ('God is with us,' 1:23) closes with the assurance that he is with them still, and will be to the end of time. This promise is not merely for the individual, but for the group. Chapter 18 verse 20 assures them as they gather in his name that he is in their midst. Without his presence and empowering, they could never even contemplate world mission. When the Lord commands, he enables. And his enabling is his presence.[33] ...The presence and the authority of Jesus are specifically attached to his command to fulfill the Great Commission. That is what Christians in hard places like China, Russia, South Korea, Sarawak and Peru are finding, as new believers flood into their churches. It is an outward thrust that would delight the heart of Matthew.[34]

His Presence is the hope and power we need to be those people who make as their aim—as part of an authentic church—to keep the main thing, the main thing.

David Bosch said, "Mission is, quite simply, the participation of Christians in the liberating mission of Jesus, wagering on a future that verifiable experience seems to belie. It is the good news of God's love, incarnated in the witness of a community, for the sake of the world."[35] Why settle for anything less? The Lord of the Church has called, provided, enabled, and empowered all who are His for this divine adventure. He is the God of mission and when we walk with Him in His mission in his world, life will be lived in supernatural terms.

The diagram below may prompt some actions; it sets out some simple applications of how we might activate the mission instructions of Jesus from Luke 10.

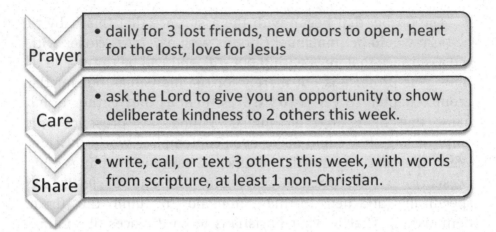

Prayer
- daily for 3 lost friends, new doors to open, heart for the lost, love for Jesus

Care
- ask the Lord to give you an opportunity to show deliberate kindness to 2 others this week.

Share
- write, call, or text 3 others this week, with words from scripture, at least 1 non-Christian.

Discussion Questions

1. Look at contrasts between the early church and the contemporary church cited by Michael Green. Which do you most strongly agree/connect with and which would you disagree with?

2. Review the section on prayer. How could you organize a group around you to put this into practice?

3. What have you found helpful to your prayer life? Commit with others to pray for three to five lost friends daily and to pray together on a regular basis.

4. When you think of evangelistic mission involving Prayer, Care, and Sharing as seen in Luke 10, how would that look:
   a. For you?
   b. Your church?

5. What changes do you need to make to be more intentional about active mission?

Notes

[1] Colossians 1:14ff

[2] Luke 24:44-49, Mark 16:15-18, John 20:19-23, Matthew 28:18-20, Acts 1:8

[3] Leslie Newbigin, *The Gospel in a Pluralist Society.* (Grand Rapids, MI: William B. Eerdmans, 1989)

[4]Kendra Creasy Dean, *Almost Christian.: What the Faith of Our Teenagers is Telling the American Church (New York: Oxford, 2010).*

[5] Michael Green, *Evangelism in the Local Church,* (London: Hodder and Stoughton, 1990), page 400ff.

[6] M. Wilcock, *The Savior of the World: The Message of Luke's Gospel: The Bible Speaks Today,* (Downers Grove, IL: InterVarsity Press, 1979), 119.

[7] E. J. Orr, *Evangelical Awakenings Worldwide,* (Chicago: Moody Press, 1975) - Hardcover, 238 pages

[8] Warren W. Wiersbe, *The Bible Exposition Commentary* (Lk 10:1), (Wheaton, IL: Victor Books, 1996).

[9] A. W. Tozer, *I Talk Back to the Devil: The Fighting Fervor of the Victorious Christian* (Wingspread, 2008).
A.W.Tozer,http://cmunki.net/articles/Tozer%20and%20Simpson%20on%20Spiritual%20Warfare.htm

[10] From a message at MissionsFest, Vancouver, 2013.

[11] Read his whole message on prayer: http://hopefaithprayer.com/prayernew/the-place-of-prayer-in-evangelism-r-a-torrey/

[12] M. Wilcock, *The Savior of the World: The Message of Luke's Gospel: The Bible Speaks Today,* (Downers Grove, IL: InterVarsity Press, 1979), 120.

[13] Christopher J. H. Wright, *The Mission of God's People: A Biblical Theology of the Church's Mission* (Grand Rapids: Zondervan, 2010).

[14] John Dickson, *The Best Kept Secret of Christian Mission: Promoting the Gospel with More Than Our Lips* (Grand Rapids: Zondervan, 2010).

[15] Gary R. Habermas, *The Historical Jesus: Ancient Evidence for the Life of Christ* (Joplin, MO: College Press Publishing, 1996).

[16] Here the Apostle Paul in his very early Christian writing (mid 50's A.D.) states that he is reminding them of the content of the gospel.

[17] Dickson, *The Best Kept Secret of Christian Mission*, 117.

[18] See Philippians 2:5-10 and 1 Timothy 2:5.

[19] See 2 Corinthians 5:21.

[20] See Ephesians 1:20-21.

[21] J. Gresham Machen, *Christianity and Liberalism*, new edition (Grand Rapids, MI: Wm. B. Eerdmans, 2009), 28ff.

[22]   Keller, http://redeemer.com/about_us/vision_and_values/core_values.html, (accessed July 9, 2013).

[23] N. T. Wright, *Mark for Everyone* (London: Society for Promoting Christian Knowledge, 2001), 4.

[24] Examples would include: 1 Cor. 15:1-8 (Peter); Acts 10:34-4 (Stephen); Acts 7:2-53 (Paul); Acts 13:16-42, and many others.

[25] Preach the Word: Essays in Expository Preaching. Lealand Ryken and Todd A. Wilson, Crossway, 2007, 108

[26] C. H. Dodd, *The Apostolic Preaching and Its Developments* (Hodder & Stoughton Ltd, 1936). Cited online: http://en.wikipedia.org/wiki/Kerygma

[27] Dickson, *The Best Kept Secret of Christian Mission*, 56.

[28] Acts 2:44, 4:32, 34, 35; 6:1

[29] See Luke 6:36, John 13:36-37; 15:12, Ephesians 4:32, Romans 15:7, 2 Corinthians 8:7-9.

[30] Dever, *The Gospel and Personal Evangelism*, 51.

[31] Wright, *The Mission of God's People*, 29.

[32] Dickson, *The Best Kept Secret of Christian Mission*, 81.

[33] M. Green, *The Message of Matthew: The Kingdom of Heaven: The Bible Speaks Today* (Leicester, England; Downers Grove, IL: InterVarsity Press, 2001), 321.

[34] Ibid., 323.

[35] David Bosch, *Transforming Mission: Paradigm Shifts in Theology of Mission* (Maryknoll, NY: Orbis Books,1991).

CHAPTER SIX

Five Things the Devil Loves in Church!

"But a man named Ananias, with his wife Sapphira, sold a piece of property, and with his wife's knowledge he kept back for himself some of the proceeds and brought only a part of it and laid it at the apostles' feet. But Peter said, 'Ananias, why has Satan filled your heart to lie to the Holy Spirit and to keep back for yourself part of the proceeds of the land? While it remained unsold, did it not remain your own? And after it was sold, was it not at your disposal? Why is it that you have contrived this deed in your heart? You have not lied to man but to God'" (Acts 5:1-4).

Recently a U.S. Supreme Court Justice stunned a journalist from the *New Yorker Magazine* when he discussed his belief in a literal devil. His comments went viral and interestingly included a reference to C. S. Lewis' book, *The Screwtape Letters*, a fictional account of demonic tactics. Can an educated and sophisticated person actually believe that a personal devil exists? According to a recent poll,[1] nearly six out of ten Americans believe in the existence of the devil. However, many people in society today think the idea of the devil is either unrealistic, unnecessary, or a leftover from medieval mythology. At the same time, our culture continues to be fascinated by dark, evil, and demonic imagery. From *The Exorcist* a generation ago, to vampires and zombies today, our culture seems to be captivated by the dark side.

If the devil cannot stop the church, he will do whatever he can to sidetrack it. If he cannot stop you from becoming part of the Church, through the new birth of God's Spirit, he will do all he can to make you an ineffective part of it.

> If the devil cannot stop the church, he will do whatever he can to sidetrack it.

The purpose in this chapter is not to develop a complete theology of the devil and the demonic realm. It is, however, our purpose to assert that the Lord Jesus and His early followers both spoke clearly about the existence of the devil and detailed some of the tactics the devil employs with God's people.

Early on in the explosive history of the church, we see an awareness of the activity of the devil in the midst of God's people. In Acts 5, there is the troubling account of deception and hypocrisy in the church that culminates in the death of two members of the community. Apparently, the fast spreading spiritual awakening that was taking place had led many people to acts of great sacrifice for the cause of Christ.

"...And with great power the apostles were giving their testimony to the resurrection of the Lord Jesus, and great grace was upon them all. There was not a needy person among them, for as many as were owners of lands or houses sold them and brought the proceeds of what was sold and laid it at the apostles' feet, and it was distributed to each as any had need" (Acts 4:33-35).

Sacrificial acts like this led many onlookers to hold these Christians in high regard. Yet the writer goes on to share some sad family news: one couple was eager to use the situation for personal gain. This temptation did not end with the early church; there is always a temptation to use Jesus for our personal ambitions. The leader of the early church, Peter, exposes both the act and the source of such behavior with these words: "But Peter said, 'Ananias, why has Satan filled your heart to lie to the Holy Spirit and to keep back for yourself part of the proceeds of the land?'"

The words of the Apostle Peter strike a profound and disturbing chord in the hearts of his first hearers and to all who take seriously the call of Christ today. Consider these implications:

- Whatever fills us is what controls us. If we are filled with the Holy Spirit, we will be led to act in ways that please the Lord. These acts will build up His Church, will encourage others, and will cause us to be more like Jesus. If, however, we are filled with anything else, we will live and act in ways that oppose the Lord. According to God's Word, it is possible to be filled with many things: bitterness, anger, greed, self, or pride. A vital question for a follower of Jesus to ask is, "is there anything that hinders the Holy Spirit from filling me?"[2]

> Whatever fills us is what controls us.

- Satan is a real being who acts and influences those he can to act in ways that oppose God's purposes. As John Stott says, "The story of the deceit and death of this married couple is important for several reasons. It illustrates the honesty of Luke as a historian; he did not suppress this sordid episode. It throws light on the interior life of the first Spirit-filled community; it was not all romance and righteousness. It is also a further example of the strategy of Satan."[3]

- It is possible to be a person in the midst of God's people and to be filled with an opposing influence! It is interesting that in the first encounter Jesus has with a gathering of God's people, the Jews, there is a person who is controlled by a demonic spirit (see Mark 1). It is possible that this man had been a leader, contributor and member for a long time, but Jesus exposes the real controlling influence in his life.

The conflict between the devil and God's people can be seen in the beginning of the human story where the serpent uses his cunning ways in attempt to stop God's creative purposes. Though he initially succeeds in getting humanity off track, God declares the ultimate outcome: the devil will be crushed. Satan's ultimate failure is assured by God's decree. Genesis 3:15 says, "I will put enmity between you and the woman, and between your offspring and her offspring; he shall bruise your head, and you shall bruise his heel."

However, the people of God, His Church, find themselves living in the period of time in which the dying serpent is still able to strike out, and with great effect. Christians need to be alert to such efforts and tactics, which distract and paralyze them, keeping the Church of Jesus from being authentic.[4] "In Christian living, as in Christian ministry, the terms are the same for us as they were for Jesus and the apostles: 'For our struggle is not against flesh and blood, but against the rulers, against the authorities, against the powers of this dark world and against the spiritual forces of evil in the heavenly realm' (Eph. 6:12). To ignore Jesus' unveiling of that enemy is to invite disaster."[5]

In the New Testament, the Apostle Peter changes the imagery of Satan the serpent, to the devil as a roaring lion. There he warns early Christians, along with all future Christians, of those tactics of the devil, which can lead to much devastation in the church.

"Be sober-minded; be watchful. Your adversary the devil prowls around like a roaring lion, seeking someone to devour. Resist him, firm in your faith, knowing that the same kinds of suffering are being experienced by your brotherhood throughout the world" (1 Pet. 5:8-9).

Peter's warning about the devil in this passage includes these vital truths:

- The devil is a malevolent being (your adversary) that is at work against what God desires in our lives. The only image we might have of a lion may be of one that is overfed and sun-drenched, lying in the local zoo. However, the first readers of Peter's warning might have pictured the horrible attacks on fellow believers that took place in the Roman Coliseum, where many Christians were literally devoured by hungry lions. "They had seen human blood dripping from the chops of lions in the gory spectacles of a Roman amphitheater."[6] Peter says not to be duped by the spirit of the age that denies the real and dangerous work of Satan, which can be very destructive within the realm of the church.

- The devil's tactics are deceptive and his actions can easily be missed. When I am helping Christians settling a dispute, such as a marriage conflict, I have found it helpful for us to remember that the primary source of this conflict, the real enemy so to speak, is not one another but the devil. Peter reminds us that the devil prowls around hidden and unseen, but he is very much at work. One of his great hopes is that we dismiss his very existence. "Presumably Satan, like a lion, may hunt by stealth as well as by terror; he could not ask for a better cover than the illusion that he does not exist, or that his comeback is merely metaphorical. Jesus Christ came to expose as well as to destroy the works of the devil."[7]

•   The way to defeat the devil's attack is to recognize his works (be watchful), to resist them, avoid them, and stand in the authority and security we have in Christ Jesus. "The danger to the Christian is not that he is helpless before the devil. He is equipped with the whole armor of God: the shield of faith will extinguish the flaming darts of the evil one. The danger to the Christian is that he will fail to resist, that he will not watch and pray, that he will not put on the whole armor of God and take the sword of the Spirit. That sword, the word of God, was the weapon Jesus used in his ordeal in the desert; it is ours to use in his name."[8]

Five Ways that the Devil Attacks Within the Church Today

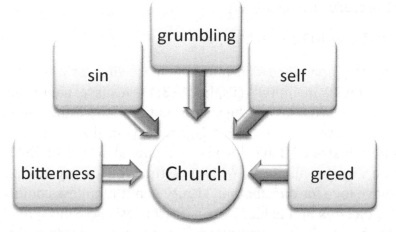

We must remember that the Church is not a building or an organization but is the gathering of people who love and serve Jesus in a locality. With this in mind, it should not surprise us that the most effective attacks will be those that happen through the actions of people who are within these local gatherings. To be sure, the church does sustain many attacks from the outside in the form of persecution, trials, and hardship, but some of the devil's most effective work is through internal means. The kinds of things that are so close to us that might go undetected in our lives may be the ones causing havoc in the church. We may go so far as to say that there are certain things that the devil inspires and loves to see in the church. When these things are present, he knows that not only is the church not a threat to him, it is also actually working for his purposes in the world! Our challenge in reviewing these five factors is to see if there are any signs of them in us personally or in the church of which we are a part. John Stott says there are two fronts on which we can expect the attacks of the enemy, from without and from within. "We have now seen that, if the Devil's tactic was to destroy the church by force from without, his second was to distract it by falsehood from within. He has not given up the attempt, whether by the hypocrisy of those who profess but do not practice, or by the stubbornness of those who sin but do not repent. The church must preserve its vigilance."9

1. UNITY & BITTERNESS

"Behold, how good and pleasant it is when brothers (God's family) dwell in unity!" (Psalm 133:1). Jesus expands on the Psalmist's words, saying the sign of authenticity in the church is unity: "A new commandment I give to you, that you love one another: just as I have loved you, you also are to love one another. By this all people will know that you are my disciples, if you have love for one another." Unity is not mindless conformity to the dictates of a leader. Nor is it to dress, act, and mimic the styles of a charismatic organizer. The unity that is refreshing and empowering is the shared purpose of mission that Christians rally around in the church.

Dylan and Janet have formed an amazing community, which has sacrificially engaged in loving the poor in one of the planet's poorest nations. What began, as a family holiday a decade ago has become the shared vision to change the lives and destiny of a region as an expression of Christ's love. It is amazing to watch them organize events, rally friends and colleagues, and mobilize resources that have changed the lives of families in whose only other prospect was destitution. Their lives have become a visual aid of that "good and pleasant" life that the Psalmist says is the fruit of unity. This kind of living is what authentic church life should look like, not simply exciting Sunday worship services, but holistic living for the glory of Jesus.

How can the devil bring ruin to the effectiveness of this community of unity? Simply by finding someone who will be the carrier of bitterness. If he can't keep you from coming to Christ, he will seek ways to keep you from effective living for Jesus. Few things are more useful to his evil purposes than un-forgiveness and bitterness. Interestingly, Jesus only mentions the church twice in all the gospels, and in one reference He speaks about this dangerous trap of un-forgiveness (see Matthew 18). The writer in Hebrews warns us with these words:

"See to it that no one fails to obtain the grace of God; that no 'root of bitterness' springs up and causes trouble, and by it many become defiled" (Heb. 12:15).

> If he can't keep you from coming to Christ, he will seek ways to keep you from effective living for Jesus.

The Peanut's cartoon character "Pig-pen" would always bring with him a cloud of stench that affected everyone around him. That's an image of the spiritual stench that hovers around those who carry with them the unwashed sins of un-forgiveness. Soon it spreads to the people around them like an infectious disease and can well destroy the work of the Holy Spirit. This is what the passage in Hebrews speaks of when it says, "Defiles many;" the fruit that is spread to others is bitter and can have all kinds of sad effects.

I well remember a person who was a source of much harm in a church where I once served. Sadly, their legacy in that church was not one of fruitfulness and the joy of knowing Jesus, but one of causing much division and pain. A former pastor of that same church later contacted me to ask if the same bitter person was still in the church, as they had been a source of pain in his time. That is not the type of legacy God wants us to leave; he has so much more that could result from our lives together. We need to ask the Holy Spirit if this is true of us: Am I harboring un-forgiveness to others in the church? Am I angry yet not seeking to resolve it with those involved? Let the revival begin with us! Let Him come in and remove that root so that there can be sweetness in our midst.

"There are few things more tragic than a church divided...yet, too often, the church is known by their bickering and division among itself, rather than churches' love for one another."[10]

Ask the Holy Spirit to search your heart and reveal if there is anyone with whom you are angry or embittered. Ask Him to give to you the humility and grace needed to resolve and heal this breach as soon as possible. Ask Him who you might need to have help you through this situation so that His church can progress in power and purpose.

2. PURITY & HIDDEN SIN

Another way the devil has effectively worked to keep the church from having its true impact in the world is through the deception that we can hide disobedience to Jesus in our lives. Hidden sin is comparable to buried landmines that mar the face of many war-torn parts of the world, their sudden detonation bringing terrible consequences to the unsuspecting. We already noted an early church example of this in the story from Acts 5 with Ananias and Saphira. This was a "big deal" in that fragile expression of the early Church, because of the potential impact their deception could have on so many others. "The story of Ananias is to the book of Acts what the story of Achan is to the book of Joshua. In both narratives an act of deceit interrupts the victorious progress of the people of God."[11]

God's plan in making us a part of His new family, the Church, is to impart to us new character that looks like His family. Christians are meant to be "little-Christs," in that they reflect the character of Jesus Christ. This does not happen automatically; it is the result of embracing the new-life power of the Holy Spirit to put to death old ways of living in us. This is the message of passages like Colossians 3: "If then you have been raised with Christ, seek the things that are above... put to death therefore what is earthly in you...." The imagery is one moving steadily toward Christ-likeness in which sins have less room in our lives.

John's first letter was written to remind Christians of their ability to resist and overcome sin in their lives and how to recover when they fail (See 1 John 1:7-2:2). However, he is also at pains to remind Christians that if sin persists in their lives, they need to question whether there has ever been a new birth.

"Whoever says 'I know him' but does not keep his commandments is a liar, and the truth is not in him, but whoever keeps his word, in him truly the love of God is perfected. By this we may know that we are in him: whoever says he abides in him ought to walk in the same way in which he walked" (1 John 2:4-6).

You may recall the story of Achan, the man who stole and buried objects for himself that were meant to be given to God's service. The result of his hidden sin was that many others were killed and wounded, a disaster for the people of God. Tragically, there are far too many stories of sin and failure in the church, particularly in leadership. Recently I was told of yet another church leadership failure, and I wanted to see if the details were accurate. When I Googled the phrase "mega church pastor scandal" I found not only the one in question, but five other scandals that were going on during the same time period! These events do much damage to the body of Christ and those around it. At times it is hard to imagine how the witness of Christ can be restored.

Rather than looking to others, we need to reflect with the Lord to see if there are things buried under our own tents. If so, we need to do whatever it takes to see God's restoration take place in our lives. This will mean repentance to the Lord and likely, confession to those involved. There is too much at stake to leave these things buried; foremost, there is the honor of our Savior, but along with that there is the integrity of our lives and relationships, which is priceless. Once uncovered, these sins need to be repented of and confession must be made as needed. Only as we walk in the light will we experience the power of Christ in authentic Christian fellowship. Once again the words of the Apostle John tell us that, "if we walk in the light, as he is in the light, we have fellowship with one another, and the blood of Jesus his Son cleanses us from all sin" (1 John 1:7).

A word about confession may be helpful. Dr. J. Edwin Orr used to say about confession, "Let the circle of the sin be the circle of confession." In other words, we need to be honest with all involved about our sin, but also to use caution to not cause others to stumble by giving too much detail where it's not needed or helpful.

> "Let the circle of the sin be the circle of confession."

John Stott offers similar advice about confession, as well as the need for church discipline when known sin is not confessed. "It is a good general rule that secret sins should be dealt with secretly, private sins privately, and only public sins publicly." Stott continues, in regard to un-confessed offences, "Churches are also wise if they follow the successive stages taught by Jesus (refer to Matthew 18). Usually the offender will be brought to repentance before the final stage of excommunication is reached. Offences, which are serious in themselves, have become a public scandal, and have not been repented of, should be judged. Presbyterians are right to 'fence the table,' that is, to make access to the Lord's Supper conditional. For, although the Lord's Table is open to sinners (who else either needs or wishes to come to it?), it is open only to penitent sinners."[12]

Ask the Holy Spirit to search your heart and reveal if there is any disobedience in your life, things, which the Lord has forbidden, and you have hidden. Ask Him to give to you the humility and grace needed to repent and confess these things. Acknowledge that hidden sin has an effect on His church and you want it cleared out. Tell Him you want the restored joy of salvation. Ask Him who you might need to help you through this situation so that His church can progress in power and purpose.

3. SUBMISSION & GRUMBLING

Throughout the history of God's people, there have been challenging issues around leading and following. As Moses set out to obey God's call to leadership, he faced many challenges to the ways in which he fulfilled that calling. Of course, leaders have flaws and don't hear the Lord perfectly, but they have to obey God's call. Every authentic church has God-given leaders who are called to seek Him and fulfill the vision and mission of God's call for that church. This also means that many of us are called to trust the Lord in following and eagerly supporting the leaders He has in place in our church. Hebrews 13:7-8 says, "Remember your leaders, those who spoke to you the word of God. Consider the outcome of their way of life, and imitate their faith. Jesus Christ is the same yesterday and today and forever." Those called to follow need to evaluate and discern if the vision of a given church is one they can support. If so, then they need to give support to the leaders in completing the work that the Lord has set before them.

The story of Korah's rebellion in Numbers 16 serves as a stark reminder of the seriousness with which God views grumbling and rebellion in those He has called to follow Him. Korah's words have been repeated and paraphrased many times throughout the history of the church. "We have a vision too, who do you think you are? We have every right to do it our way...." These are the words of a divisive person who should be avoided at all costs as they will sow seeds of division and discord that ultimately God will judge.

To be sure, a divisive person will never *claim* to be divisive and contentious for they always consider their agenda a worthy cause. It would be wise to examine the history of these people and what they have done before in previous settings. Do they have a reputation of division or of serving hearts? Therefore, Christians need discernment as they look at what others *do*, not only at what they *say*. Scripture has many warnings about these wolves in the flock. Consider these two passages:

"As for a person who stirs up division, after warning him once and then twice, have nothing more to do with him, knowing that such a person is warped and sinful; he is self-condemned" (Titus 3:10-11).

"I appeal to you, brothers, to watch out for those who cause divisions and create obstacles contrary to the doctrine that you have been taught; avoid them. For such persons do not serve our Lord Christ, but their own appetites, and by smooth talk and flattery they deceive the hearts of the naive" (Rom.16: 17-18).

One contemporary church leader notes that trust is a vital issue for an authentic church: trust in the Lord and those whom He calls to lead. "When there is distrust among people in the church, especially among leaders, division is almost certain. On one hand, leaders have the God-ordained responsibility to be trustworthy and above reproach (1 Tim. 3:2, 10; Titus 1:6). On the other hand, church members have a God-ordained duty to honor and submit to their leaders, which requires a level of trust (1 Thess. 5:12-13, 1 Tim. 5:17, Heb. 13:7, 17).[13] The enemy loves to sow distrust of leadership and looks for willing participants for his cause.

Another way the enemy distracts the church from its kingdom mission is to focus a group of Christians on their pet topic or theological hobbyhorses and to sow distrust in others who also share the name of Christ. In his book *The Screwtape Letters*, C. S.

Lewis imagined an experienced devil, Screwtape, writing letters to his young nephew, Wormwood, on the best practices for moving people toward hell's objectives and away from the side of the devils' enemy, the Lord. This is some of the advice given to Wormwood about the kind of church to direct the patient to in order to, keep him ineffective:

"Any small clique, bound together by some interest which other men dislike or ignore, tends to develop inside itself a hothouse mutual admiration, and towards the outer world, a great deal of pride and hatred which is entertained without shame because the 'Cause' is its sponsor and it is thought to be impersonal. Even when the little group exists originally for the Enemy's own purposes, this remains true. We want the Church to be small not only that fewer men may know the Enemy but also that those who do may acquire the uneasy intensity and the defensive self-righteousness of a secret society or a clique. The Church herself is, of course, heavily defended and we have never yet quite succeeded in giving her all the characteristics of a faction; but subordinate factions within her have often produced admirable results, from the parties of Paul and of Apollos at Corinth down to the High and Low parties in the Church of England."[14]

Again, the challenge to us is not to look around and see to whom this message might apply, but to search our hearts and see if this is true in us. We need to humbly ask the Holy Spirit to reveal to us any unacceptable attitudes He wants to expose in our hearts. The Lord may well have put leaders over us that He will use to address corrective issues in our lives. We will not always agree and understand the directions that confront us in the life of the church; however, if we believe the leadership is prayerful, scriptural, and obedient, we need to stay the course and see what God can do. Meanwhile, we can ask the Lord to show us if there are things that He wants to address in our lives.

As Psalm 139:23-24 says:

> "Search me, O God, and know my heart!
> Try me and know my thoughts!
> And see if there be any grievous way in me,
> and lead me in the way everlasting!"

4. SERVANTHOOD & SELFISHNESS

What happens when you order a "regular cup of coffee" at Starbucks? You will receive a free blank stare! That is what happens to me when I customarily try it just for effect. Why? Because there is no such thing! In fact, the company claims that a customer can order up to 87,000 different variations of a cup of coffee! This is an important part of the Starbucks strategy: engaging the customer in a personalized process that allows them to be in control. They will pay a premium to do so, and will even become loyal customers. Marketers know that our culture is very self-focused and have used this insight to engage customers in a myriad of ways.

While this may be valuable in the marketplace in which we live, these values are not ones that should drive the Church. A self-focused experience is not what the Church is meant to be about. There are some attempts to run customer-driven churches in our culture, but these efforts are a failed understanding of the intent of Jesus. Now these trends are not new—they go right back to the first disciples of Jesus who began to look for ways to make His cause something that would serve them. Mark's Gospel tells of one such occasion and the resulting lessons:

"And James and John, the sons of Zebedee, came up to him and said to him, 'Teacher, we want you to do for us whatever we ask of you.' And he said to them, 'What do you want me to do for you?' And they said to him, 'Grant us to sit, one at your right hand and one at your left, in your glory.' Jesus said to them, 'you do not know what you are asking. Are you able to drink the cup that I drink, or to be baptized with the baptism with which I am baptized?' And they said to him, 'We are able.' And Jesus said to them, 'The cup that I drink you will drink, and with the baptism with which I am baptized, you will be baptized, but to sit at my right hand or at my left is not mine to grant, but it is for those for whom it has been prepared.' And when the ten heard it, they began to be indignant at James and John. And Jesus called them to him and said to them, 'You know that those who are considered rulers of the Gentiles lord it over them, and their great ones exercise authority over them. But it shall not be so among you. But whoever would be great among you must be your servant, and whoever would be first among you must be slave of all. For even the Son of Man came not to be served but to serve, and to give his life as a ransom for many'" (Mark 10:35-45).

> The devil is fine with a church in which everyone is striving to accomplish his or her own agenda.

The honesty of the biblical record is refreshing–such obvious flaws and failures revealed in the lives of the original disciples! If the Bible were the kind of fabricated myth that was generated to support some man-made religious movement—as it is often portrayed in popular culture—it would not contain these types of records, but rather glossy accounts of success.

The devil is fine with a church in which everyone is striving to accomplish his or her own agenda. James and John had the nerve to ask Jesus to grant them their wishes of co-leadership in His new movement. They clearly had not understood the call to "come and die," to use the words of Bonhoeffer. Instead, they hoped He would give them anything they wished. Notice that Jesus re-defines for them what leadership values are in His kingdom and church. His Church was to be a place of following the Master who came into the world and lay down His life so that we might live. This then is to be seen in His people, a people who are not demanding their own way, which is devilish, but offering himself or herself to serve Him.

One of those present at the scene of that kingdom power-grab was Peter. Peter was in fact, along with the others, offended by the brothers (likely because they too wanted their personal agendas fulfilled by Jesus). Many years later, Peter would write with the strongest of warnings about this type of self-seeking spirit in the Church and, he would warn about the dangers of those who would embody it. "These are waterless springs and mists driven by a storm..." (2 Pet. 2:17).

"That is, they have their own wants and pleasures, and they justify indulging those desires by raising queries about those points of theology which condemn them. These are the people Peter has already described as 'experts in greed,' 'mists driven by a storm,' 'slaves of depravity' (2 Pet. 2:14, 17, 19). Although these people may present themselves as sophisticated and knowledgeable, having delicate qualms and posing courageous questions about the more difficult elements of Christian teaching, they are in reality, driven by their greed and disobedience. It is sin, not sophistication, which is in the driving-seat, and the false teachers are merely *following*."[15]

Once again, we need to ask the Lord to search our hearts and reveal to us whether these may well have become attitudes within us. If the earliest Christians needed the revelation of God to show them and deliver them, it is not impossible that we too may need the same. "It may amaze us that the disciples could be so slow to grasp 'what it was all about.' We need not spend too long on that line. Jesus' teaching in these verses shows discipleship as a self-denying, self-risking, self-giving part of lowly service for the redemption of the world. Yet so much of Christian life as one can now observe it is about gaining a secure position in society, inviting others to join us where we are, doing little to change the structures of our political and social life, thus lending our support to structures which oppress the poor and needy at home and abroad, and largely leaving it to preachers and full-time evangelists to spread the good news about Jesus. We are not (mostly!) as crass as the disciples in jockeying for seats of power in the kingdom, but by much more subtle behavior we show how little we grasp what it means to be disciples of a crucified Lord who gave his life as a ransom for many."[16]

5. GENEROSITY & GREED

The devil is always attempting to counterfeit God's genuine currency as a way to distract the church from its true power and resources. Another of his ploys is the spread of what could be called the "gospel of Simon" in the lives of many Christians. This is the kind of religious message about selfishness that is seen in Acts 8, in the story of a man named Simon. He appears to be a genuine convert among many others in a fresh move of God. However, he embraces his newfound faith as a means of personal financial growth and prosperity. The account in Acts 8 reads:

"Now when Simon saw that the Spirit was given through the laying on of the apostles' hands, he offered them money, saying, 'Give me this power also, so that anyone on whom I lay my hands may receive the Holy Spirit.' But Peter said to him, 'May your silver perish with you, because you thought you could obtain the gift of God with money! You have neither part nor lot in this matter, for your heart is not right before God. Repent, therefore, of this wickedness of yours, and pray to the Lord that, if possible, the intent of your heart may be forgiven you'" (Acts 8:18-22).

Regrettably, this "gospel of Simon" is still in the Church twenty centuries later. At times, it is because of ignorance about the cost of discipleship, while in other instances there is a blatant message preached about personal benefits as the rewards for those who claim them "in faith." The words of Jesus that welcome all to come to Him (Matt. 11:28ff) are also words which warn us that this journey is one of obedience and hardship and may include homelessness (Matt. 8:18ff). This selfish spirit, "covetousness which is idolatry," is far too common in the use of our resources. Few Christians actually give a proportion of their income to the cause of the gospel, deceived into believing it does not matter. The words of Haggai 1 are still a relevant challenge: "Is it a time for you yourselves to dwell in your paneled houses, while this house lies in ruins?"

An excessive form of this "gospel of Simon" has been called "the prosperity gospel." It is so-called because some have taught that God's eternal gift is focused on a material prosperity. In fact, it has become such a significant snare in the contemporary church that a global movement for authentic faith, the Lausanne Movement, felt the need to write a theological response to it. The theological position paper included these words:

"We affirm the miraculous grace and power of God, and welcome the growth of churches and ministries that demonstrate them and that lead people to exercise expectant faith in the living God and his supernatural power. We believe in the power of the Holy Spirit.

"*However, we reject as unbiblical the notion that God's miraculous power can be treated as automatic, or at the disposal of human techniques, or manipulated by human words, actions or rituals.*

"We affirm the biblical teaching on the importance of hard work, and the positive use of all the resources that God has given us–abilities, gifts, the earth, education, wisdom, skills, wealth, etc. And to the extent that some Prosperity teaching encourages these things, it can have a positive effect on people's lives. We do not believe in an unbiblical asceticism that rejects such things, or an unbiblical fatalism that sees poverty as a fate that cannot be fought against.

"*However, we reject as dangerously contradictory to the sovereign grace of God, the notion that success in life is entirely due to our own striving, wrestling, negotiation, or cleverness. We reject those elements of Prosperity Teaching that are virtually identical to 'positive thinking' and other kinds of 'self-help' techniques.*

"*We are also grieved to observe that Prosperity Teaching has stressed individual wealth and success, without the need for community accountability, and has thus actually damaged a traditional feature of African society, which was commitment to care within the extended family and wider social community.*[17]

On the other hand, when the power and truth of God's offer of new life and cleansing of the old life (the gospel) touch a person, transformation takes place. One of the clear signs of an authentic Jesus-encounter in the life of a person will be seen in their attitude to belongings. When a money-oriented taxman named Zacchaeus met Jesus, a whole new approach to belongings was seen in his life (Luke 19:1-10).

This new attitude is heard in the challenge of the Apostle Paul's words to the church in Corinth as he highlights this generous attitude that was being expressed through other churches.

"We want you to know, brothers, about the grace of God that has been given among the churches of Macedonia, for in a severe test of affliction, their abundance of joy and their extreme poverty have overflowed in a wealth of generosity on their part. For they gave according to their means, as I can testify, and beyond their means, of their own accord, begging us earnestly for the favor of taking part in the relief of the saints" (2 Cor. 8:1-4).

Paul seeks to correct the church at Corinth by holding up the example and effects of grace on the lives of others who met Jesus. "Their liberality (generosity) was not of themselves naturally, but of God's grace bestowed on them, and enabling them to be the instrument of God's 'grace' to others." [18]

Jeffrey was a contractor and had grown up in church but would now confess he knew very little of authentic Christian discipleship. He tells of a spiritual experience that changed his whole direction. It was one of those unusual and unexpected events when the Lord stirs someone to get their attention. The basic details of his story

> "...the line dividing good and evil cuts through the heart of every human being."
>
> - Solzhenitsyn

deal with his sense of God exposing his greedy lavish lifestyle and complete neglect of kingdom values when viewed on a global scale (one might argue this includes all North Americans).

As a result, Jeffrey asked the Lord to give him a new start and allow him to become a conduit of funds for God's work in the world. He determined before the Lord that he would tithe a certain amount beginning that year and double it every year if God would enable him to do so. The last time I spoke to him a few years ago, he was planning to give $460,000 for the work of the gospel, up from $230,000 the previous year. While his story is unique, it illustrates the kind of spirit that can make an authentic church powerful in its witness in the world. In addition, when a group of believers begins to trust God in this way, they will be witness to amazing signs and wonders from the Lord, because they are pursuing His agenda.

CONCLUSION

The devil trembles when the church is authentic, living in its full inheritance and advancing the kingdom of God through holy lives and obedience. There are legions of ways the enemy would want to distract the church from its God-given mission and inheritance. As already mentioned, our temptation is to search for these attitudes in other churches or other Christians; however, the real place for inquiry needs to be in our own hearts. The words of Aleksandr Solzhenitsyn are a candid reminder, "If only it were all so simple! If only there were evil people somewhere insidiously committing evil deeds, and it were necessary only to separate them from the rest of us and destroy them. But the line dividing good and evil cuts through the heart of every human being. And who is willing to destroy a piece of his own heart?"[19]

The greatest, most under-used weapon to overcome that the Lord has given us is prayer. Once again, the advice of Screwtape serves as a vivid reminder of the power of prayer.

"The best thing, where it is possible, is to keep the patient from the serious intention of praying altogether. When the patient is an adult recently re-converted to the Enemy's party, like your man, this is best done by encouraging him to remember, or to think he remembers, the parrot-like nature of his prayers in childhood. In reaction against that, he may be persuaded to aim at something entirely spontaneous, inward, informal, and unregularised; and what this will actually mean to a beginner will be an effort to produce in himself a vaguely devotional mood in which real concentration of will and intelligence have no part. One of their poets, Coleridge, has recorded that he did not pray 'with moving lips and bended knees' but merely 'composed his spirit to love' and indulged 'a sense of supplication.' That is exactly the sort of prayer we want; and since it bears a superficial resemblance to the prayer of silence as practiced by those who are very far advanced in the Enemy's service, clever and lazy patients can be taken in by it for quite a long time. At the very least, they can be persuaded that the bodily position makes no difference to their prayers; for they constantly forget, what you must always remember, that they are animals and that whatever their bodies do affects their souls. It is funny how mortals always picture us as putting things into their minds: in reality our best work is done by keeping things out.

"If this fails, you must fall back on a subtler misdirection of his intention. Whenever they are attending to the Enemy Himself we are defeated, but there are ways of preventing them from doing so. The simplest is to turn their gaze away from Him towards themselves. Keep them watching their own minds and trying to produce feelings there by the action of their own wills. When they meant to ask Him for charity, let them, instead, start trying to manufacture charitable feelings for themselves and not notice that this is what they are doing. When they meant to pray for courage, let them really be trying to feel brave. When they say they are praying for forgiveness, let them be trying to feel forgiven. Teach them to estimate the value of each prayer by their success in producing the desired feeling; and never let them suspect how much success or failure of that kind depends on whether they are well or ill, fresh or tired, at the moment."[20]

Finally, Samuel Chadwick's words are as relevant today as when he first penned them: "Satan dreads nothing but prayer. His one concern is to keep the saints from praying. He fears nothing from prayer-less studies, prayer-less work, prayer-less religion. He laughs at our toil, he mocks our wisdom, but he trembles when we pray."[21]

Discussion Questions

1. A vital question for a follower of Jesus to ask is, "Is there anything that hinders the Holy Spirit from filling me?"

2. Read Numbers 16. What are the lessons there about division and grumbling? What can we do when we hear a fellow believer speaking about their church leadership in disparaging ways?

3. Of the five attitudes mentioned in this chapter, which are most likely to flourish in my heart? What would combative prayer look like in my life?

4. Read the quote from *Screwtape* near the end of the chapter. What important lessons does Lewis convey there?

5. What is one point from the chapter that resonates most with you and why?

Notes

[1] YouGov Poll 2013: 57% of Americans believe in the devil.

[2] For Luke, in declaring that Ananias *kept back* part of the money for himself, chooses the verb *nosphizomai*, which means to "misappropriate" (BAGD). The same word was used in LXX of Achan's theft, and in its only other New Testament occurrence it means to steal. We have to assume, therefore, that before the sale Ananias and Sapphira had entered into some kind of contract to give the church the total amount raised. Because of this, when they brought only some instead of all, they were guilty of embezzlement.

[3] John R. W. Stott, *The Message of Acts: The Spirit, the Church & the World* (Leicester, England; Downers Grove, IL: InterVarsity Press, 1994), 108-109.

[4] But the fact that Satan has been cast down from heaven and knows that his time is short makes him, in a sense, a more formidable adversary. His fury against the Lord and his kingdom is the more intense. He may threaten the church from within, masquerading as an angel of light. He may rage from without, using the fire and sword of persecuting tyrants. But the Christian knows that "The God of peace will soon crush Satan under your feet."

[5] Milne, *The Message of John: Here is Your King!*, 133.

[6] Clowney, *The Message of 1 Peter: The Way of the Cross,* 213.

[7] Ibid., 214.

[8] Ibid., 215.

[9] Stott, *The Message of Acts: The Spirit, the Church & the World*, 112.

[10] Mark Driscoll and Gerry Breshears, *Vintage Church: Timeless Answers to Timely Questions* (Wheaton, IL: Crossway Books, 2008)..

[11] Stott, *The Message of Acts: The Spirit, the Church & the World*, 109.

[12] Ibid., 112.

[13] Driscoll and Breshears. *Vintage Church.*

[14] C. S. Lewis, *The Screwtape Letters* (New York: HarperCollins, 1942).

[15] R. C. Lucas and C. Green, *The Message of 2 Peter & Jude: The Promise of His Coming* (Leicester, England; Downers Grove, IL: InterVarsity Press, 1995), 129-130.

[16] D. English, *The Message of Mark: The Mystery of Faith* (Leicester, England; Downers Grove, IL: InterVarsity Press, 1992), 182-183.

[17]http://www.lausanne.org/en/documents/all/twg/1099-a-statement-on-the-prosperity-gospel.html

[18] Robert Jamieson, A. R. Fausset, and David Brown, *Commentary Critical and Explanatory on the Whole Bible* (Oak Harbor, WA: Logos Research Systems, Inc., 1997).

[19] Aleksandr Solzhenitsyn, *The Gulag Archipelago 1918-1956*, (New York: Basic Books, 1997).

[20] Lewis, *The Screwtape Letters*, chap. 2.

[21] Milne, *The Acts of the Apostles*, 142.

CHAPTER SEVEN

Bowling Alone: Does Membership Have Its Benefits?

"Through the work of the apostles, many God-signs were set up among the people, many wonderful things done. They all met regularly and in remarkable harmony on the Temple porch named after Solomon. But even though people admired them a lot, outsiders were wary about joining them. On the other hand, those who put their trust in the Master were added right and left, men and women both" (Acts 5:12-14, The Message).

Some of the angriest letters I have ever received came to me when I was a young pastor. My colleagues and I made, what seemed at the time, a rather reasonable decision for the circumstances, which we had observed. After we had been pastoring a year or two in an established church, we noted that there were many people who were on our membership list who no longer attended the church. Several people had moved to other parts of the country and others simply stopped coming. We drafted a pleasant letter wishing them well and conveyed that we hoped that they had found a new church community of which to be a part. In addition, we noted that we would be dropping them from our church membership list as they were no longer active there.

Now there wasn't any smoke from the edges of the first letter in the return mail, but its fiery contents certainly got my attention, as did several other letters! The initial letter was filled with "Who do you think you are?" and, "I'll have you know that my family..." type of stuff. As I tried to make sense of the writer's anger, hurt, and the threats that came with it, I realized we had come a long way from a biblical view of belonging to a church or church membership. Over the years I have made a few observations in regards to the topic of church membership or officially belonging to a church. There are those people:

* Who insist on being church members who are never involved in church life

* Who are involved in serving, but do not want to become members of the church

* Who want to belong to a church but do not believe that membership is a biblical concept

> In the early church... it was pretty clear who belonged, who did not, and why.

In the early church, as we see in the above passage from Acts 5, it was pretty clear who belonged, who did not, and why. As the exciting story of that earliest church unfolds, there are some crucial observations that we shouldn't

CHURCH: IS THERE AN APP FOR THAT? | 115

miss. Notice in the passage cited above, at least three truths that are evident from an initial reading:

1. The church was nothing less than the gathering together of those people who had had a genuine encounter with Jesus: "They all met regularly and in remarkable harmony...." This is the foundation of an authentic church. To be sure, there may need to be organizing principles, governance, and structures, but they are only the scaffolding to the growing organism.

2. Gathering together was an exciting prospect for Christians because God was active in their midst: "many God-signs were set up among the people, many wonderful things done." Too much of what we call "church" today is void of the eager anticipation of what God might do as we gather to worship Him.

3. It was clear to all that some people belonged and that others did not: "outsiders were wary about joining them." Why were they wary? Likely because they could see that belonging to this group meant an ultimate change of allegiance, and it had a high personal cost. This is, of course, what Jesus means when He says that if you want to follow me there is no room for other agendas or multiple diversions in life that are short of the gospel (Luke 9:52ff). Put another way: there can be no authentic church life without authentic Christians.

Before proceeding much further, it may be helpful to clarify a distinction between what theologians have termed the "universal Church" and the "local church." The universal Church is the sum of all those Christians around the globe who are members of God's family through faith in Christ. The universal Church will only be able to gather together in that last day at the return of Christ. (The Apostles' Creed calls this church "catholic" with a small "c" as distinct from the Roman Catholic Church, which is a sub-set of the universal Church.) The local church refers to a distinct gathering of baptized Christians in a given locale who worship, serve, and witness together for the glory of God. All Christians, saved by faith in the work of Christ, are members of the universal Church. It is my hope here to demonstrate that all Christians should be engaged members of a local church.

Who is In and Who is Out?

If we are going to have an experience of an authentic church we need to be clear about who can participate and why. A note in passing, I have chosen to use the term "belonging" to a church as a clarifying synonym to the term "membership." While I believe the concept is a biblical one, the term membership, in my experience, has too many confusing or negative connotations in our culture.

In his provocative book, *Bowling Alone: The Collapse and Revival of American Community,*[1] Harvard University professor Robert Putnam notes that the number of people who participate in bowling has actually increased over the previous twenty years. However, the number of people who are members of bowling leagues has decreased. He demonstrates that since the 1960s, there has been a massive decline in memberships for all sorts of organizations. Some of the reasons for this decline inc-- lude family structure, age, suburban life, television, computers, women's roles, urban sprawl, and the increasing pressures of time and money.

As the culture around us moves away from the commitments of belonging to groups and organizations, how are Christians to respond? If the church is just another one of the many community groups vying for membership, in order to "keep the program going," then there is certainly a cause for deep concern. However, while there are many examples of churches devolving into that sort of quagmire, that is not the essential nature of an authentic church. The grounds for belonging to a church, which are found in the Bible, are quite different from those of many worthwhile community organizations.

SAINTS, BROTHERS, AND BELIEVERS

One way to explore what the grounds are for belonging to a church is to examine some of the words used to describe those who belonged to the early church. There are three particular words in the Bible that deserve consideration: *saints, brothers, and believers.*

Saints: For many of us, the term connotes a stain-glass window sort of figure from the past, one who is possibly part fiction and part reality, a mythical person quite unlike us. Perhaps we think of one of the inspiring missionaries to India like the Roman Catholic Mother Theresa or the Protestant Amy Carmichael, people whose lives where inspiring examples of loving the "least of these." Yet, this term "saint" is the term that is used of ordinary Christians in the Bible. Those who belonged to the Church were all called saints, not because of extraordinary actions which they had achieved, but because they had embraced the extraordinary actions of Jesus Christ on their behalf. The word "saint" in the original Greek New Testament is *hagios* and is found in its plural form (saints) sixty-one times and its singular form (saint) once – "greet every saint."

The word "saint" means to be 'holy, different from others, not common, but set aside for a special use.' In the Bible we learn that God is holy (1 Pet.)–that means He is *Wholly Other*, different than the creation, different from humanity–all-powerful and altogether different than all that we observe. When something other than God is called holy, it means it has been set apart for

His special purposes. The land of promise was called holy, furniture in the temple was called holy, and most remarkably, people are called holy because they have been set apart by God's grace to serve His purposes. They are Christ's "dedicated people."

Because they are saints—those who have been set apart from the world by Christ's saving work—Christians live differently than the world around them. They are invited to live in the constant presence of Jesus Christ, hungry for His word and direction. The Apostle Peter says that these "saints" will be seen by the world around them as oddballs or weirdoes, though the kinder word used is "sojourners" (1 Pet. 2:11). "Because Christians are strangers in the world, they are considered to be strange in the eyes of the world (1 Pet. 4:4). Christians have standards and values different from those of the world, and this gives opportunity both for witness and for warfare."[2]

Saints are seen as different people in virtually every domain of life. Pick almost any area of living: sexuality, money, time, career... Christ's people will manifest a different life, because a different spirit than that of this world indwells them.

My friend, David, is a man who is one of those oddballs! His first career was actually as an athlete, playing what Canadians consider the only true sport: hockey! To be honest, the first time I was taken to an NHL hockey game, I thought I had been time-warped into a Roman Coliseum! The violence and fighting that happens as part of the game took me by total surprise, not to mention the howling and jeers of the fans...but I digress. David came to know Christ during his career in hockey, which led him to make many life changes. After sports, he became a lawyer and progressed in that field for several years. I met him shortly after he moved his family to my city to take a very significant position for a large corporation.

Shortly after joining our home Bible study group, he announced that he had quit his job, having only been there a few months. It was clear that this was not an easy decision and would have major consequences on his family's life. When asked what had happened, David explained that he had been made aware of illegal practices in the company, practices which he addressed with the CEO. He was told not to worry about the details, to keep up the required work and to take home a big paycheck. He relayed to our group that this was not an option for a follower of Jesus, and he had told the corporate leader that the office could keep the big paychecks. Other executives in the company could not understand his actions and even assured him that he was "safe" to continue, but that is not what saints do. He would trust his true boss to provide even at great personal cost to his career and family.

There are many people in church every Sunday that express quite a different life than one of being set-apart. They may well have a membership card but lack that inner life which willingly embraces the cost of following Jesus. Their questions are along the lines of, "Do I have to do this?" "Can I give only this much of my time, money, talents?" "Why should I should I serve or attend or read or...?" These are signs of unregenerate people who are not ready to belong to a church. They may be "pillars of the church," but remember often a 'pillar' is that which holds things up, blocks the view, and seems to always be in the way!

Brothers: In the book of Acts alone, the term "brothers" (*adelphos*) is used fifty-two times to describe those who belong to the Church. It signifies that both men and women have become a part of a new family and have new family ties. (The use of a masculine term is in no way meant to exclude sisters! We can see this as shorthand for women and men who have been given a new family status because of Jesus being excluded on our behalf on the cross.) This family gives them a new inheritance, a new caregiver, new bonds of love, a new community, and new values just to name a few. As one writer clarifies, this term is distinctly Christian:

"One day when Jesus was teaching a group of disciples in a house in Capernaum, he was told that his brothers were waiting to talk to him outside, but he answered that he was already with his brothers, for 'whosoever shall do the will of my Father which is in heaven, the same is my brother.' As in everything that Jesus said, his point was simple but profound. Physical brotherhood is not as important as spiritual brotherhood, and whatever a man's earthly family may be, his true brothers (and sisters) are the ones who have the same Father in heaven. For this reason the word "brethren" was used by the followers of Jesus when they spoke of one another... But most often in the New Testament we see that this word (*adelphos* in the Greek) was used by Christians when they wanted to refer to another member of the church.... The word 'Christian,' which is more commonly used than 'brother' now, was actually coined by non-Christians, and it was not normally used in the Church. H. B. Hackett observes, 'It was by this name [*adelphos*] that Christians usually spoke of each other. The name Christian (literally little Christs) was merely used to describe them objectively, that is, from the Pagan point of view, as we see from the places where it occurs, namely Acts 11:26, 26:28, and 1 Pet. 4:16.'"[3]

One implication of this term "brothers" and its significance is really what it says to "sisters." To say that women in the ancient world were under-valued would be a massive understatement. Many cultures devalued women as objects to be used and discarded or even offered as gifts to the gods. For instance, girls at very young ages in a Hindu culture were commonly offered as a "bride to the gods" (e.g. a ritual prostitute) by their parents. Their reasons may have been of economic status, convenience, but often were religious; it inevitably meant a life of shame and sorrow. In fact, this ancient practice was only outlawed in India in the 1980s. I recently read an article on human trafficking that explains something of this practice:

"In India, the devadasi (day-vah-dah-see) system, a Hindu practice of temple prostitution, has existed more than 5,000 years, says David Dass, executive director of the India Gospel League. In the state of Karnataka where he and his wife live, starving families dedicate hundreds of girls each year to the goddess Yellamma. The children are forced to begin a life of prostitution at age 11 or 12.

"'From the very beginning, they're being exploited as babies,' says Annette Romick, a humanitarian aid worker in India. 'Then, when they hit maturity, their bodies are exploited by men. Even when their bodies are no longer desirable to men, they are still exploited and abused because that stigma is on them. They can never escape from it. It's a trap that they're stuck in; it's a living hell that they're experiencing.'

"The word devadasi literally translates to 'god's female servant.' Parents usually choose to dedicate their daughters as infants to the goddess Yellamma in hopes of gaining the goddess' favor or easing a financial burden."[4]

The message that God's family is a place where both men and women are valued and given equal status was then—as it is now—good news! Young girls are made in God's image and are not objects or playthings to be used and discarded by our sick and broken world. They are to be treated with dignity, value, and care, as sisters who sit at the table of God's family.

Jesus astounded His hearers by elevating a woman who had become something akin to a sex-trade worker to family status in Luke 7:44-50:

"Then turning toward the woman he said to Simon, 'Do you see this woman? I entered your house; you gave me no water for my feet, but she has wet my feet with her tears and wiped them with her hair. You gave me no kiss, but from the time I came in she has not ceased to kiss my feet. You did not anoint my head with oil, but she has anointed my feet with ointment. Therefore I tell you, her sins, which are many, are forgiven—for she loved much. But he who is forgiven little, loves little.' And he said to her, 'Your sins are forgiven.' Then those who were at table with him began to say among themselves, 'Who is this, who even forgives sins?' And he said to the woman, 'Your faith has saved you; go in peace.'"

Our Western culture has lost sight of the radical nature of this truth, which we now assume was simply the fruit of the enlightenment that all reasonable people would acknowledge. However, in reality it is the legacy of the gospel, entering a culture and transforming it to reflect God's truth of inherent human value, which is the true reality. There are many other implications to explore around the word "brothers," but the point here is that it was this truth of becoming a part of God's family that made belonging to a church a valued position.

> When God's family is divided and fractured, the church ceases to be an authentic church until healing and restoration comes.

The devil knows just how vital this family tie is in the church and therefore has done some of his greatest work to destroy it. When God's family is divided and fractured, the church ceases to be an authentic church until healing and restoration comes.

Believers: The term "believers" is less commonly used of those who belong to a church in the Bible than saints or brothers, but it certainly has significance. It indicates someone who accepts the apostolic testimony about Jesus as the only Savior and Lord of all life. The term "belief" today is generally seen as little more than accepting a given proposition. For example, someone might well say, "I believe that Aspirin can relieve headache pain." That level of belief is useful but will not provide any change of condition. To believe—in the biblical sense of the word—adds a deeper level of action based on the facts that are known. This deeper level of belief would be expressed in words like, "I had a headache, but it's gone now because I took some Aspirin to cure it." There are some distinct characteristics of believers in the early church, which should be noted:

a. They believed *in* Christ Jesus not just about Him.

There are some people in the church today that have been, in the words of one Christian writer, "justified by thought, but not justified by faith." In other words, they know what it is to be "churched," but not converted. They have correct ideas about Jesus, but they have not met Him nor trusted Him in a personal way. This leads to a crucial difference in whether or not they will experience the wonder of being a part of an authentic church. The Apostle John tells us that one result of Jesus turning water into wine was that some began to understand who He was and did the wisest thing possible: they trusted Him as their Maker and Savior to do His miraculous and transforming work in their lives. They saw the need to believe in Him, not just about Him.

"This, the first of his signs, Jesus did at Cana in Galilee, and manifested his glory. And his disciples believed in him" (John 2:11).

This was more than the simple "level 1" sort of faith, affirming correct ideas about Jesus. It was that "level 2" sort of faith that was mixed with placing their trust in Him, which led to a life-changing experience of Him.

Just as with a climbing, a large group can be instructed about the safety and thrill of rappelling down a tower's side. However, only those who believe at the level of putting their full trust in the rope can actually experience it.

Jesus gives a chilling warning about authentic faith, which is believing in Him and not just about Him, in the parable about sheep and goats:

"When the Son of Man comes in his glory, and all the angels with him, then he will sit on his glorious throne. Before him will be gathered all the nations, and he will separate people one from another as a shepherd separates the sheep from the goats. And he will place the sheep on his right, but the goats on the left" (Matt. 25:31-33).

The sheep are not saved because they did good things, but they did good things because they shared His life, which became theirs by believing in Him. The goats did not do or even see what Jesus would do ("Lord, when did we see you hungry and not feed you...?") because they had NO spiritual life; they simply believed about Him.

b. Their believing led them to *Behave* like Jesus.

Early in my life as a Christian, I discovered the majestic statement of Jesus found in John 14:6: "I am the way, and the truth, and the life. No one comes to the Father except through me." This verse was greatly challenging to me. It was so comprehensive and leaves no doubt about the uniqueness of Jesus. At the same time, I find these words comforting as they help me to see the completeness of Jesus for every need in life. Some years later I made a much more provocative discovery in the same chapter, six verses later where Jesus says:

"Truly, truly, I say to you, whoever believes in me will also do the works that I do; and greater works than these will he do, because I am going to the Father" (John 14:12).

Jesus' words seem to challenge those who believe in Him, His followers, that they will do even greater things than He did. After first reading that verse I wondered if He could possibly mean that. I am now convinced that Jesus meant what He said in this promise. He wanted those early believers and all subsequent ones to wrestle with how this could be. How could anyone do what Jesus did, and especially greater things? He seems to intend that the "greater things" are not so much mightier miracles but on a much larger scale. His works would not be confined to one small landmass in first century Palestine but would be done around the planet and throughout time. But how?

The answer to the 'how' question comes as we read on in John's gospel. We read in John 14:25-26:

"These things I have spoken to you while I am still with you. But the Helper, the Holy Spirit, whom the Father will send in my name, he will teach you all things and bring to your remembrance all that I have said to you."

> "Will God ever ask you to do something you are not able to do? The answer is yes--all the time!"

Jesus tells of a new, powerful, and personal presence of God that each person can know, the Holy Spirit, who comes so we can live the Jesus life. What Jesus made possible on the cross, the Holy Spirit wants to make actual in our lives.

As Henry Blackaby says:

"Will God ever ask you to do something you are not able to do? The answer is yes—all the time! It must be that way, for God's glory and kingdom. If we function according to our ability alone, we get the glory; if we function according to the power of the Spirit within us, God gets the glory. He wants to reveal Himself to a watching world."[5]

The gifts and the fruit of the Holy Spirit enable us to live and act in the likeness of Jesus. Character and conduct are the genuine signs of being filled with the Holy Spirit. The questions we need to ask of ourselves and our church community are: Are we filled with the Holy Spirit? If not, why not? Are we seeing Jesus do His works in our midst? If not, why not? Imagine a church where the members believed confidently in Jesus to act through them and behaved more and more like Jesus as a result of dependence upon Him. Would that make a difference in the community, workplace, homes, and the margins of our world? We need to remember that this is only possible if we are a Spirit-filled and Jesus-centered people.

This is what we should expect because of the powerful presence of God within us, both individually and corporately.

"Those in whom the Spirit comes to live are God's new Temple. They are, individually and corporately, places where heaven and earth meet."[6]

> "Those in whom the Spirit comes to live are God's new Temple. They are, individually and corporately, places where heaven and earth meet." N. T. Wright

Janet[7] is a bright university student who considers herself "spiritual but not religious." She was recently invited to participate in a home fellowship group from our church. She attended for several weeks and joined in the experience of Bible study, worship, sharing, and prayer. After about her fourth week of attending the group, she eagerly reported to the group that since they had prayed for her the previous week she was now free of chronic pain! Someone said, "Wow, praise the Lord" in mild disbelief, and Janet raised her hands and declared, "Yes, praise the Lord!" She does not fully know all that the discovery means yet, but she is seeing the works of Jesus being done.

c. The believers *Belonged* to Jesus.

In the ancient world when someone fell into debt, there were few options to solve their financial situation. There were no government checks, debt reduction services, or bankruptcy protection policies to help them. One solution was to become a servant (*doulos*) of someone else who would pay off the outstanding debts. In return, the individual would give a number of years of service to the one who released them from debt. On occasion, such a positive relationship would develop between master and servant that the debtor would choose to remain a server for life, becoming a "bond-servant."

It is remarkable to see that this was the normal picture for the early believers. Jesus was not an optional or added extra in life; He was their absolute Master. It was quite common to reference believers as *servants or bondservants* in that way in the early church.

"For do I now persuade men, or God? Or do I seek to please men? For if I still pleased men, I would not be a bondservant of Christ" (Gal. 1:10 NKJV).

"Epaphras, who is one of you, a bondservant of Christ, greets you..." (Col. 4:12 NKJV).

"Paul, a bondservant of God and an apostle of Jesus Christ..." (Titus 1:1 NKJV).

Believers in the Bible who submitted to Jesus and lived as bondservants prepared to obey His will and listened carefully to His words. They identified themselves as *belonging* to Jesus.

Early Christians would gladly identify themselves this way, because this is how their Lord Jesus was identified. In Philippians 2, Paul says Christ "...emptied himself, by taking the form of a servant, being born in the likeness of men. And being found in human form, he humbled himself by becoming obedient to the point of death, even death on a cross" (vv. 7–8).

We should not be able to read these words without a sense of awe and wonder stealing over our hearts. If anyone ever had the right to insist on His rights, it was the Lord Jesus. But His concern for others (those whom the Father had given Him) was such that He refused to insist on His rights. He did not cling to His divine prerogatives, but willingly laid aside all the trappings of His glory and took our humanity."[8]

An ironic contrast to the bondservant image of following Jesus is seen in the story of the first Czar of Russia, Ivan the Terrible. He was in love, and the object of his affection was Sophia who would not marry him unless he was baptized in the church. Eventually Ivan compromised. He would be baptized as a member of the church, but he would hold his sword above the baptismal waters! This would enable him to fulfill marital pressure and maintain his personal ambition. He could still fight, kill, conquer and ravage others just as before. While Ivan's story seems ridiculous, it is not far from what continues to happen in our own day. To belong to the church of Jesus, it must mean we are willing to serve Him as Lord and Master who has the right to direct and guide our lives. In fact, Jesus makes it abundantly clear that this is what He calls us to.

"And calling the crowd to him with his disciples, he said to them, 'If anyone would come after me, let him deny himself and take up his cross and follow me. For whoever would save his life will lose it, but whoever loses his life for my sake and the gospel's will save it. For what does it profit a man to gain the whole world and forfeit his soul? For what can a man give in return for his soul? For whoever is ashamed of me and of my words in this adulterous and sinful generation, of him will the Son of Man also be ashamed when he comes in the glory of his Father with the holy angels'" (Mark 8:34-38).

Ivan's story does beg the question—is there something that I have held out of the water? Is there a part of my life that I hold in reserve from the rule of Jesus?

As we will see in the coming chapter, God has designed some remarkable things for those who are a part of an authentic church. However, before exploring those benefits, it was crucial that we clarify who could actually belong to such a church. Saints, brothers, and believers: these are the qualities and qualifications of those who can belong to a church.

Discussion Questions

1. Read the opening passage again (Acts 5:12-14). What are two to three key ideas that strike you?

2. Is there something you see in this chapter that requires obedience and if so, what would it look like for you to obey it?

3. How would you decipher what the Bible says about being a saint, from popular ideas in culture?

4. What is one issue raised in this chapter that you want to explore more?

5. If you were asked about who could be a church member what would you say, and what scripture would you refer to?

Notes

1 See further: "Bowling Alone: The Collapse and Revival of American Community" by Robert Putnam: http://en.wikipedia.org/wiki/Bowling_Alone

2 Warren W. Wiersbe, *The Bible Exposition Commentary* (1 Pe 1:1). (Wheaton, IL: Victor Books, 1996).

3 Michael Marlowe, (bible-researcher.com) cites H. B. Hackett, *Dr. William Smith's Dictionary of the Bible*, revised and edited by Professor H. B. Hackett, vol 1 (Boston, 1881), 329.

4 Baptist Press, January 2012: http://www.bpnews.net/printerfriendly.asp?ID=36941

5 Henry T. Blackaby, *Experiencing the Spirit: The Power of Pentecost Every Day*

6 Wright, *Simply Christian: Why Christianity Makes Sense.*

7 This is a real person; I changed the name and details to honor an ongoing personal journey.

8 Roger Ellsworth, *Opening up Philippians, Opening Up Commentary* (Leominster: Day One Publications, 2004), 37.

CHAPTER EIGHT

Worship:
More Than Singing Songs

*"Worthy are you, our Lord and God, to receive glory and honor
and power, for you created all things, and by your will they
existed and were created" (Rev. 4:11).*

There are few things in the church as neglected, misused,
fought-over, misunderstood, or trivialized as the great calling
and privilege of worship. The reasons for this reality are
complex and multifaceted, but undoubtedly find many of their
roots in what the Apostle John called the Christian's battle with
the world, the flesh, and the devil. We live in a rebel environment
(the world) that opposes the centrality of the Lord Jesus and His
honor. We wrestle against unconquered inner desires (the
flesh), which do not naturally fall in line with God's purposes. In
addition, there is a spiritual adversary (the devil) who will do all
he can to prevent the people of God from enjoying all that is

rightfully theirs as God's Church on earth. However, scripture gives us some hope-filled insights and directions into proper worship and how God's people can be transformed through worshipping Him.

"After this I looked, and behold, a door standing open in heaven! ...Around the throne were twenty-four thrones, and seated on the thrones were twenty-four elders, clothed in white garments, with golden crowns on their heads. From the throne came flashes of lightning, and rumblings and peals of thunder, and before the throne were burning seven torches of fire, which are the seven spirits of God, and before the throne there was as it were a sea of glass, like crystal.

"And around the throne, on each side of the throne, are four living creatures, full of eyes in front and behind: the first living creature like a lion, the second living creature like an ox, the third living creature with the face of a man, and the fourth living creature like an eagle in flight. And the four living creatures, each of them with six wings, are full of eyes all around and within, and day and night they never cease to say,

"'Holy, holy, holy, is the Lord God Almighty, who was and is and is to come!'

"And whenever the living creatures give glory and honor and thanks to him who is seated on the throne, who lives forever and ever, the twenty-four elders fall down before him who is seated on the throne and worship him who lives forever and ever. They cast their crowns before the throne, saying,

"'Worthy are you, our Lord and God,
to receive glory and honor and power,
for you created all things,
and by your will they existed and were created'"
(Rev. 4:1-11).

These words from John's heavenly vision allow us to see some celestial glimpses of heavenly worship. Here we discover that "this is what worship is all about. It is the glad shout of praise that arises to God the creator and God the rescuer from the creation that recognizes its maker, the creation that acknowledges the triumph of Jesus the Lamb."[1] This is the ideal as seen in John's heavenly vision and what all who are in Christ are destined for; regrettably it is not what all who are in Christ experience in the church on earth. However, that does not need to be the case. It is possible to align ourselves more closely to the ideal seen in the heavenly realm. We can be helped in this by exploring what the Bible tells us about what worship is, why we are called to worship, and how we can worship Jesus more meaningfully.

WHAT IS WORSHIP: PICTURES & WORDS

Perhaps you have been asked after a church service, "What did you think of the worship this morning?" You will realize that more than likely the question is about your opinion of the music style. This has become the common use of the word *worship* in many church contexts today. However, it is not what the word in its original context means, nor is it a useful or authentic way to think about what it means to be worshippers.

A Worship Lesson From An Agnostic Hermit:

Paul lives a quiet life on the edge of a small village in the northern woods of Ontario, Canada, in a simple house that he built, one without running water or an indoor bathroom. This home shelters him through the extreme seasons including months of temperatures of -40 during the deep of winter. He has travelled the world as an explorer for an oil company, working in the deserts of Libya and in the High Arctic of Canada, in places where few other humans have ever been. Paul is a bachelor in his eighties, with a large world-view and insight from having lived a very unique life. He has strong ideas about politics, the price of oil, materialism, and wood stoves. His gentle laugh, great conversation, and passion for the game of cribbage make it easy to spend hours together.

I met Paul when staying nearby in the comfortable cottage of a friend. After a few roadside chats, I invited him over for coffee and soon we were discussing matters of faith and belief. Paul had befriended some local nuns who, now in their eighties, have been a part of his local community for decades. He had little formal church experience but still had his opinions about what is what. As we discussed the church in particular, Paul had some observations about why he found the church difficult to take seriously. He talked of some of the hurdles that had kept him from feeling he could engage in a church. These included greedy evangelists who bilk the simple out of their savings to build massive empires for themselves. Sadly, there have been several of these folks in the history of the church (perhaps Judas was their patron saint). We could agree that this sort of behavior was not what Jesus modeled or called His followers to. Of course, no discussion of the church is complete without beating on a few "hypocrites," who I know the church is full of, being a recovering one myself!

Strikingly, the main reason Paul confided that he finds no need for the church is because, in his words, "Sometime back they dropped the Latin!" Awkward pause, "umm... *carpe diem*" I agreed! Actually, I could not have been more surprised. He certainly was not a devout Roman Catholic, and he had little exposure to a mass. So I asked him what he meant by that. Paul told me he had visited a church in the past decade or two and was disappointed to see "a shortened service, for those who can't pay attention for one hour, a couple of young beatniks strumming their guitars instead of the organ, and most of the great language missing from the service." Then, his muse, which I found so deeply resonant, "I just feel that worship should be something above us, not dumbed down for everyone–that's all." Paul added, "Look it isn't working anyway; they think it will attract people, but it hasn't–they are still leaving the church." His words, "worship should be something above us" are reminiscent of A. W. Tozer who said that, "Worship is to feel in your heart and express in some appropriate manner a humbling but delightful sense of admiring awe and astonished wonder and overpowering love in the presence of that most ancient Mystery, that majesty which philosophers call the First Cause but which we call Our Father Which Art in Heaven."[2]

Picture and Words

The Bible gives us a few pictures of heavenly worship to help us imagine some of the eternal realities of worship, in passages such as Isaiah 6 and Revelation 4. These pictures allow us to sense some of the grandeur of God and how His mighty presence affects the creatures of His making. There is an overwhelming sense of awe, "And I said: 'Woe is me! For I am lost; for I am a man of unclean lips, and I dwell in the midst of a people of unclean lips; for my eyes have seen the King, the LORD of hosts!'" (Isa. 6:5). There is also is also a humbled recognition of the other-ness of God, "Worthy are you, our Lord and God…" (Rev. 4:11). God is central to everything in worship and those in His presence are awed by His worth and grandeur.

One way to better understand worship is to see what the word meant to the original readers and hearer. There are three root words (and a number of variants) used in the New Testament, which combined, instruct us about authentic worship.

a. Proskuneo – Means *to show submission*. There are two words combined to form this word, *pros*, which means, "to move toward" and *kuneo*, which means "to kiss." It originally carried with it the idea of subjects falling down to kiss the ground before a king or kiss their feet. It can be used to mean: to fawn, crouch toward, pay homage, do reverence to, to adore. This is the most common of the three words and it occurs fifty-nine times in the New Testament.

When Princess Elizabeth was crowned queen of England, her husband the Duke of Edinburgh bowed and kissed her hand. This was not the kiss of a husband, but the kiss of a loyal subject who was demonstrating his loyal submission and commitment to the ruling monarch. Worship is the response of loyal subjects to their sovereign who deserves their complete loyalty, love, and devotion. Our worship and worship gatherings are to be a place that will re-kindle the divine romance.

b. Sebomai – means *to show devotion or reverence, hold in awe*, and it is used ten times in the New Testament. This devotion or submission is displayed through hearing and obeying God's word from the heart: joyful obedience. "In Mt.15.8-9 Jesus accused the Pharisees and Scribes of error, quoting Isaiah 29.13, he said, '...In vain do they *sebomai (worship)* me, teaching teachings which are the commandments of humans.' The reason Jesus gave for their empty (vain) sebomai was, '[Their] lips respect me, but their heart is far from me.' That is, their heart (devotion) to Jesus was false, because they verbally claimed to follow God's commandments, but showed a lack of respect for him by following their traditions instead. They showed a lack of devotion for God because their heart was far from God. Sebomai is the opposite of this, a true showing of respect for God out of one's heart."[3]

c.   Latreuo – means *to offer religious service of respect.* It is used twenty-one times in the New Testament. In the Old Testament, this religious service denoted serving rituals toward God in times like the Passover feast or the duties of the priests in the Tabernacle and Temple. However, in the New Testament "Christians are called to *latreia* (worship) by offering their bodies (themselves) as living sacrifices. 'A word long associated with Mosaic rituals is re-defined by Paul to refer to Christian living...a word that once only referred to specified rituals is transformed by Paul to refer to daily sacrificial living by a Christian.'"[4] Worship in the New Testament is a lifestyle, a 24/7 reality seen in lives that increasingly synchronize with godly living through God's grace.

These pictures and words about worship in scripture paint a scene that refers to all of life. God's people submit, surrender, and serve Him with their whole lives. Worship has left the building so to speak, and permeates every area of life. "...Worship is being significantly de-institutionalized, de-localized, de-ritualized. The whole thrust is being taken off of ceremony and seasons and places and forms; and is being shifted to what is happening in the heart—not just on Sunday, but every day and all the time in all of life."[5] Worship is not just about going to a certain location and doing certain rituals on a regular basis. It is a response to God's greatness and grace to surrender ourselves to God and give Him the offerings called for now that Christ has offered Himself as the perfect offering for us. Namely, offering ourselves (Rom. 12:1-2),

> These pictures and words about worship in scripture paint a scene that refers to all of life.

offering our praise (Heb. 13:15), offering our resources (Heb. 13:16), and offering our gifts to others in the body of Christ (1 John 4:16-19).

William Temple summarized Christian worship like this: "Worship is the submission of all our nature to God: to quicken the conscience by the holiness of God; To nourish the mind with the Truth of God; to purge the imagination by the beauty of God; to open up the heart to the love of God and to surrender the will to the purpose of God."[6]

WHY WORSHIP: REASONS & EFFECTS

A young man would understandably tell his fiancée the things that he has come to love about her. As they have come to know one another, her worth has become greater in his estimation and, he delights to tell her of just how true this is. In an infinitely greater measure, when mere mortals begin to glimpse the greatness of God and His works, the most reasonable response of the hearts should be to declare to God the discoveries of His greatness. We can hear such wonder in the words of the Psalmist who says in Psalm 8:

O Lord, our Lord, how majestic is your name in all the earth!
You have set your glory above the heavens.
Out of the mouth of babies and infants,
you have established strength because of your foes, to still the enemy and the avenger.
When I look at your heavens, the work of your fingers, the moon and the stars, which you have set in place,
What is man that you are mindful of him,
and the son of man that you care for him?

Worship is 'Worth-Ship"

The English word *worship* has its root in the idea of declaring God's worth. This is what the elders in heaven declare, "Worthy are you, our Lord and God, to receive glory and honor and power, for you created all things, and by your will they existed and were created" (Rev. 4:11). The primary reason that we worship God is that He is worthy of it. We recognize, as His creatures, that He as our maker deserves our praise, love, and obedience. "Worship is what we were created for. This is the final end of all existence—the worship of God. God created the universe so that it would display the worth of His glory. And He created us so that we would see this glory and reflect it by knowing and loving it with all our heart and soul and mind and strength."[7] The writer to the Hebrews focuses this worship even more finely onto the person of Christ Jesus, also referring to Psalm 8, "...you have crowned him with glory and honor, putting everything in subjection under his feet" (Heb. 2:7-8). We worship God supremely because He is worthy of worship. In addition to God being worthy of worship there are other complimentary reasons that should encourage our worship.

> The English word *worship* has its root in the idea of declaring God's worth.

Worship is Reasonable

The book of Romans is an in depth exploration of all that God has done through the work of Jesus Christ to rescue His rebel world. After explaining God's wonderful actions on our behalf for eleven chapters, Paul says there is only one reasonable response to all that God has done for us: to become people who are whole-life worshippers. This response of worship he says is not only the most reasonable thing to do, but it will help us to see that He has our best in mind and will prove it in our lives.

"So here's what I want you to do, God helping you: Take your everyday, ordinary life—your sleeping, eating, going-to-work, and walking-around life—and place it before God as an offering. Embracing what God does for you is the best thing you can do for him. Don't become so well adjusted to your culture that you fit into it without even thinking. Instead, fix your attention on God. You'll be changed from the inside out. Readily recognize what he wants from you, and quickly respond to it. Unlike the culture around you, always dragging you down to its level of immaturity, God brings the best out of you, develops well-formed maturity in you" (Rom. 12:1-2, MSG).

This reasonable whole-life worship is God's call to offer ourselves; the word *parastasi* means a complete and final offer. We must settle, once and for all, which side we will be on, the world's or the Lord's. Sitting on the fence is both unstable and painful! God's promise is that He will transform those who are His worshippers. We might recognize the word "metamorphosis" and think about the miracle of change that transforms caterpillars into butterflies. "This word *transform* is the same as *transfigure* in Matthew 17:2. It has come into our English language as the word 'metamorphosis.' It describes a change from within. The world wants to change your mind, so it exerts pressure from without. But the Holy Spirit changes your mind by releasing power from within. If the world controls your thinking, you are a *conformer*; if God controls your thinking, you are a *transformer*."[8] This transforming process will prove something to us, and to a watching world, that God's will is good, acceptable and perfect.

> "If the world controls your thinking, you are a *conformer*; if God controls your thinking, you are a *transformer*." -

Worship is Effective

Something happens in the spiritual realm when God is worshipped. Acts 4:31 gives an example of what we might call a spiritual seismic shift, "And when they had prayed, the place in which they were gathered together was shaken, and they were all filled with the Holy Spirit and continued to speak the word of God with boldness." It is as if there is a flag raised for the kingdom of God that enables His rule and power to have greater freedom among those gathered to worship. Psalm 22:3 says the Lord inhabits the praises of His people.

Worship wars are not unique to the contemporary church; we find the first one in the opening chapters of Genesis. There is the sad account of two brothers who come to worship, a fight ensues and one is mortally wounded at the hands of the other. This tumult prevents the advance of God's saving grace and advances the turmoil of Satan's chaos.

> *"Worship wars* **are not unique to the** contemporary church; we find the first one in the in the opening chapters of Genesis."

This is why the devil has always opposed authentic worship and will do all he can to keep God's people from it or at least distract and divide them regarding it.

It is no surprise that the first conflict in the ministry of Jesus is a challenge in the area of worship. Satan knows how much is at stake and seeks to corrupt even the Son of God, if possible, in regard to proper worship. The account is found in Luke 4 where the writer records that Jesus was tempted by the devil in the wilderness. There are three temptations that are lessons to us regarding distractions in worship. They are the:

- Sensual – "make stones bread"—appeals to physical needs of the body and emotional satisfaction that comes from it. The temptation is to turn worship into a pursuit of a spiritual buzz for us and our needs, rather than a focus on the Lord Jesus.

- Sensational – "top of temple"—this high point was ninety feet above the valley of Hinnom–this spectacular action will "wow" lots of people, as if pleasing the crowd is the object of the exercise. Sometimes worship is diluted down to simply whatever things that will draw a crowd and falls far short of the ideals that bless God.

- Spiritual power – "taken to a high mountain"–from this point, one could see ten kingdoms in Jesus' day. The temptation was to seek spiritual power in illegitimate ways. The devil tempted Jesus with the offer to "worship me and you can have authority over all of these."

Worship Transforms

We are to worship the Lord because He is worthy of it, yet in living as a worshipper we find too that we are changed by the One we worship. Isaiah tells of his transforming experience of worship which exposed his unclean heart and unworthy motives. He also shares that in the encounter of worship he experienced God's mercy and was re-deployed in life with new purpose.

"I saw the Lord sitting upon a throne, high and lifted up; and the train of his robe filled the temple... 'Woe is me! For I am lost; for I am a man of unclean lips, and I dwell in the midst of a people of unclean lips; for my eyes have seen the King, the Lord of hosts!'

"Then one of the seraphim flew to me, having in his hand a burning coal that he had taken with tongs from the altar. And he touched my mouth and said: 'Behold, this has touched your lips; your guilt is taken away, and your sin atoned for.'

"And I heard the voice of the Lord saying, 'Whom shall I send, and who will go for us?' Then I said, 'Here I am! Send me.' And he said, "Go..." (Isa. 6:4-8).

> "One of the primary laws of human life is that you become like what you worship." - N.T. Wright

God's gift to His people in worship is His transforming power, to make them more and more like Himself, to restore the damaged image in which they are made. Yet there is a real danger in that God's creatures, people made in His image, will chose to worship something other than their creator and thereby become less and less of whom they were meant to be. As N. T. Wright explains, "When human beings give their heartfelt allegiance to and worship that which is not God, they progressively cease to reflect the

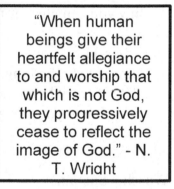

> "When human beings give their heartfelt allegiance to and worship that which is not God, they progressively cease to reflect the image of God." - N. T. Wright

image of God. One of the primary laws of human life is that you become like what you worship; what's more, you reflect what you worship not only to the object itself but also outward to the world around. Those who worship money increasingly define themselves in terms of it and increasingly treat other people as creditors, debtors, partners, or customers rather than as human beings. Those who worship sex define themselves in terms of it (their preferences, their practices, their past histories) and increasingly treat other people as actual or potential sex objects. Those who worship power define themselves in terms of it and treat other people as collaborators, competitors, or pawns. These and many other forms of idolatry combine in a thousand ways, all of them damaging to the image-bearing quality of the people concerned and of those whose lives they touch."[9] This is why God sets boundaries for us and instructs that He alone is to be worshipped, for as our maker He knows what is best and what will bring about transformation, healing, and glory.

No one but you, Lord
Can satisfy the longing in my heart
Nothing I do, Lord
Can take the place of drawing near to you

Only you can fill my deepest longing
Only you can breathe in me new life
Only you can fill my heart with laughter
Only you can answer my heart's cry

Father, I love you
Come satisfy the longing in my heart
Fill me, overwhelm me
Until I know your love deep in my heart[10]

Worship Sustains

On the course of a marathon race, runners encounter aid stations that offer them water, energy-drinks, nourishment, cheers, and encouragement. These stations are wonderful places that are vital for the runners to continue and finish their course. In authentic churches, worship gatherings are the aid-stations of encouragement, strengthening, and nourishment that enable the community of Christ to carry on and sooner or later, finish well. Worship is first given to God for His glory and yet it is for us as well, in the sense that by God's grace we are renewed as we give Him our praise and worship. Worship is meant to be a celebration of the all-sufficient One who has given all for His people - those who respond to His invitation to come to Him. Authentic churches are communities of worship that enable Christians, God's pilgrim people, to be refreshed and renewed in order to finish their journey.

> So the community of the cross is a community of celebration …
> ceaselessly offering to God through Christ the sacrifice of our praise and thanksgiving.
> - John Stott

"The Christian community is a community of the cross, for it has been brought into being by the cross, and the focus of its worship is the Lamb once slain, now glorified. So the community of the cross is a community of celebration, a Eucharistic community, ceaselessly offering to God through Christ the sacrifice of our praise and thanksgiving. The Christian life is an unending festival. And the festival we keep, now that our Passover Lamb has been sacrificed for us, is a joyful celebration of his sacrifice, together with a spiritual feasting upon it."[11]

HOW WE WORSHIP

In Samuel Beckett's play "Waiting for Godot," the characters come and stand at the appointed place where they expect to meet "Godot." A messenger boy comes and explains that Godot won't be coming this day, but will tomorrow evening. The next night, Vladimir and Estragon again meet near the tree to wait for Godot. Despite their hope and expectation, Vladimir and Estragon continue to wait without any encounter. Shortly after, the messenger boy enters and once again tells Vladimir that Godot will not be coming. After he leaves, they decide to leave and they do not move as the curtain falls, ending the play. Church for many people can feel like that place under the tree. People are in a place of anticipation and even conversation. The curtain is falling and still there is no sign of Godot.

In preparing a research project on the factors behind the exodus of a large portion of the millennial generation from the church I was struck by one particular finding.[12] While there are multiple factors behind this generational exodus (which, in a secularizing culture, includes social pressures, poor efforts at discipleship, family breakdown, and a perceived irrelevance), one factor was quite remarkable in its own right. Many respondents indicated their reason for departing from church was "the absence of wonder."[13] It seems they have had an experience like the characters Vladimir and Estragon. It is possible to make our worship gatherings a polished production, with great attention to detail, and yet find that God, "that most ancient mystery" is nowhere to be found. Hungry souls come in hopes of connecting with their creator, but instead receive principles, programs, and the promises of more next week. The longing for encountering God eventually fades as hopes of His appearing are dashed on the rocks of showmanship, entertainment, polished liturgy, or a personality cult. Authentic churches will pray and desire that God Himself has room to move among His people. The voice of Jesus needs to be heard by all His people in the clear teaching of His word, in Christ-centric music worship and in the spaces of reflection and silence, which are a crucial listening place of His gathered people. Indeed, worship should be something that is "above us," an experience of the presence of our majestic holy God.

If only we could turn to a passage in the Bible and find a clear prescription, or how-to outline for what corporate worship should look like, perhaps there would be a lot less confusion in the church on the matter. Thankfully, God has not done that for us in scripture, which in fact, would have limited our freedom of expression and restricted Christian worship to boundaries that are exclusive of some people rather than including them. Instead, as we read the scriptures we find priorities that guide worship in every culture, age, language, era, and ethnicity without restricting it to certain cultural forms, such as that of first century Palestine. In John 4, there is the account of Jesus meeting a woman at a well. The account is filled with numerous truths about Jesus, about human brokenness, and about the restoration that Christ came to bring. It is here that Jesus elevates the status of this particular woman, and in fact all women, by choosing her to reveal a staggering new understanding about authentic worship. He helps her and all who come after her to see that worship is not about geography, ancestry, or language, but that God is looking for those who will worship Him "in spirit and truth." "...In the New Testament there is a stunning indifference to the outward forms and places of worship. And there is, at the same time, a radical intensification of worship as an inward, spiritual experience that has no bounds and pervades all of life."[14]

"Jesus said to her, 'Woman, believe me, the hour is coming when neither on this mountain nor in Jerusalem will you worship the Father. You worship what you do not now; we worship what we know, for salvation is from the Jews. But the hour is coming, and is now here, when the true worshipers will worship the Father in spirit and truth, for *the Father is seeking such people to worship him*. God is spirit, and those who worship him must worship in spirit and truth'" (John 4:21-24).

Jesus liberates us from dull religious duty and invites us into a dynamic and life-giving experience–worship in spirit and truth. Authentic worship is empowered by the Holy Spirit and expressed through the human spirit. It is focused on Jesus who is the truth and is an outflow of those who have aligned their lives with His truth. Bruce Milne writes, "The spiritual nature of God (*God is spirit*) means self-evidently that we cannot relate to God satisfactorily in physical terms. He is invisible and intangible and hence beyond our immediate sense-apprehension. For God to be known and focused by us, thus making worship possible, he must take initiative to disclose himself to us. This he has done initially in the Old Testament scriptures (verse 22, the Jews 'know' whom they are worshipping). But the further and fuller revelation of God is now at hand in the Son who makes the Father known (1:18). Hence, we reach the same conclusion. True and satisfactory worship is worship offered in and through Jesus Christ; only through the truth he embodies, and the Spirit he imparts, can we know God and worship him."[15]

With these words about Spirit and Truth, the stage is set for a new experience of worship in which we can engage. And while there is not a specific format for every worship gathering to be found in the Bible, there are specific actions that can be seen in the worship of the early church. We would do well to make sure that these are included in our own experiences of worship.

WORSHIP: EAT, PRAY & READ

EAT: Food and celebration appear in the ministry of Jesus as a place of fellowship and worship (John 2, Mark 3, 7 etc.). This practice continues to be normative in the infant church. "And day by day, attending the temple together and breaking bread in their homes, they received their food with glad and generous hearts" (Acts 2:46). It appears that a practice in the early church was corporate meals followed by communion together. As Stott comments to this regard, "the definite article in both expressions (literally, 'the breaking of the bread and the prayers') suggests a reference to the Lord's Supper…although almost certainly at that early stage as part of a larger meal… ."[16] Eating continued to be a part of worship as the young Church spread, as evidenced by correction given in the church at Corinth (1 Cor. 11).

Eating was more than a potluck; it was a shared meal and shared lives that found its greatest focus in the celebration which may be known to us variously as Communion, The Lord's Supper, The Breaking of Bread, or The Eucharist. Jesus gave His followers this revised passover-esque celebration as a means of refreshing their memories and renewing their experience of God's grace whenever they gathered for worship. Whether our celebration is a simple regular reminder with a few believers together in a living room, or an elaborate event that fully rehearses the gospel for all involved, eating is to be a part of our worship. Detailed instruction can be found in 1 Corinthians 11 and is worthy of greater reflection. The instruction given there is a "timely reminder that Christian worship in Corinth was of a more informal nature, took place (in all probability) in private homes, incorporated both liturgical and spontaneous elements, and was not confined to one hour's devotions in a specially-constructed building which remained virtually unused for the rest of the week."[17] It was part of the ebb and flow of a worshipping community and we too can expect to see the Lord Jesus do wonders and signs in our midst when we worship Him in this way.

Many churches have been re-discovering that scriptural imperative that worship should include a regular celebration of the gospel meal. Those who have confined it to irregular patterns in their worship are overlooking a scriptural command and are poorer as a result.

PRAY: Another aspect of worship found in the life of the early church is prayer. Whether spoken or sung, corporately or individual, words were offered to the Lord of heaven and earth to celebrate His greatness and to call on His graciousness. The disciples were attracted to this aspect of Jesus' life and asked Him to teach them to pray. Without doubt, this group of religiously immersed people had heard many prayers and knew how to say their own prayers. However, they wanted to know more about the way in which Jesus prayed. This request led to Jesus giving what is often called the Lord's Prayer. Without expounding the many wonderful truths of this prayer, we will simply note here its corporate voice.

"Pray then like this:
Our Father in heaven,
hallowed be your name.
Your kingdom come,
your will be done,
on earth as it is in heaven.
Give us this day our daily bread,
and forgive us our debts,
as we also have forgiven our debtors.
And lead us not into temptation,
but deliver us from evil. (Matt. 6:9-13, emphasis added).

On hearing these words, the early followers of Jesus would have understood that one aspect of worship is to pray together in unity as God's new family gathered on earth. The periods of history that have seen great movements of spiritual renewal have always been accompanied by Spirit-empowered, united prayer. Worship that pleases God and empowers His people will include corporate prayers.

Authentic churches are those that have found ways to make corporate prayer an active and engaging part of their worship. This may be the reclaiming of some ancient forms of corporate prayer such as those found in historic liturgies. It may mean establishing prayer stations that are thoughtfully prepared to help teach worshippers to pray more widely. It may involve prayer walking in our community and learning to declare the wonders of our God over our community and seek that His kingdom may come. One group I have been a part of meets for one hour on top of a large hill above our city to praise God and pray for the welfare of our city. Wouldn't it be wonderful for a coming generation to experience prayer as one of the most refreshing and renewing aspects of its corporate life?

The Apostle Paul encouraged the churches in the area of Colossae with respect to their lives as churches; this included a call to prayer. "Continue steadfastly in prayer, being watchful in it with thanksgiving. At the same time, pray also for us, that God may open to us a door for the word, to declare the mystery of Christ, on account of which I am in prison" (Col. 4:2-3). Dick Lucas comments, "To *continue steadfastly (in prayer)* is to persevere, and to persevere is to busy oneself with the task in hand, rather like that energetic little widow who gave her local magistrate no rest. A characteristic mark of the earliest Christians is their devotion to intercessory prayer.... It is of great interest that the first duty of the Christians in Colossae was to open their mouths in prayer."[18]

> Prayer is one of those topics that can provoke feelings of failure and awkwardness, but it need not.

Prayer is one of those topics that can provoke feelings of failure and awkwardness, but it need not. What if instead we chose to find creative ways to re-embrace this part of worship and to use the many gifts of the body to grow together in wonderful avenues of corporate prayer? There is such a broad pallet of color and a large canvas in prayer that the possibilities are limitless. One recent prayer experience I enjoyed with a group was a focused time of prayer, which began with engaging worship music videos. The setting was warmed with candles, and the seating was inviting. After a time of focusing on the Lord in praise, we were invited to allow the Lord to guide us to pray for people in our lives that had a special need to know God's grace. Remarkably, I found that many names and faces came to mind and, it was easy to join others in lifting our requests for these loved ones to Jesus. Places were provided for writing names and scriptures on a prayer wall as a tactile way to present our request to God. Finally, we were given time to "soak" in His presence in a space of quiet and worshipful music. This united prayer time took preparation, but it was appealing and inviting for continued growth in prayer and it seemed that the time went so quickly.

READ: Returning once again to that proto-typical church in Acts, we see that another element of Christian worship is the adherence to God's revealed truth as it is found in the canon of scriptures. Acts 2:42 says, "And they devoted themselves to the apostles' teaching and the fellowship, to the breaking of bread and the prayers." In short, their devotion to the Apostles' teaching is reverence for the Bible as God's revelation of action on earth. As Stott says, "Since the teaching of the apostles has come down to us in its definitive form in the New Testament, contemporary devotion to the apostles' teaching will mean submission to the authority of the New Testament. A Spirit-filled church is a New Testament church, in the sense that it studies and submits to New Testament instruction. The Spirit of God leads the people of God to submit to the Word of God."[19] Again, we can explore some fresh new ways to make the Bible a central part of our worship. Certainly, this needs to include preaching which unfolds the truths that are declared in the Bible, but it can mean more for us. Being a community that reads the lectionary or a Bible reading plan and sharing discoveries we are making there can be marvelously unifying. One fellowship I know of gathers in coffee shops in small groups during the week for Bible reading,

> "Our hearts are restless, until they can find rest in you."

journaling, and prayer. The result has been an explosion of discovery, obedience, guidance and worship among them.

Reading scripture as part of worship is essential as N. T. Wright comments, "Telling the story, rehearsing the mighty acts of God: this is near the heart of Christian worship.... We know God through what He has done in creation, in Israel, and supremely in Jesus, and what He has done in His people, and in the world through the Holy Spirit. Christian worship is praise of this God, the one who has done these things, and the place we find the God-given account of these events is of course scripture: the Bible."[20]

CONCLUSION:

As we gather for worship we will want to be sure the elements of Eat, Pray, and Read are aspects of our worship. At the same time, we want to prepare so that our worship gatherings are engaging, vibrant, and our own hearts are ready for encountering the Lord.[21] We don't have to settle for the dull routine that is often accepted as public worship. Once again Stott's reminder regarding worship in the earliest church in Acts is fitting. "It is right in public worship to be dignified; it is unforgivable to be dull. At the same time, their joy was never irreverent. If joy in God is an authentic work of the Spirit, so is the fear of God. 'Everyone was filled with awe' (v.43), which seems to include the Christians as well as the non-Christians. God had visited their city. He was in their midst, and they knew it. They bowed down before him in humility and wonder. It is a mistake; therefore, to imagine that in public worship, reverence and rejoicing are mutually exclusive. The combination of joy and

> "Our worship, incredible as it may appear in our eyes, matters immensely to him." - Bruce Milne

awe, as of formality and informality, is a healthy balance in worship."[22]

The Lord our maker made us for worship, that is the universal longing of the human heart and, it is the design of the infinitely wise God. As Augustine said, "You have made us for yourself, and our hearts are restless, until they can find rest in you."[23] The people of God are God's new temple on earth that are being built together as the place where worship is most meaningful and honorable. "They are the kind of worshippers...the Father seeks (John 4:23), and nothing so encourages our approach to him than to realize this. Our worship, incredible as it may appear in our eyes, matters immensely to him. He gave his only Son to make it possible. To you...he has said, 'seek my face!'"[24]

Discussion Questions

1. Reflecting on the original words that are translated as worship. How might you explain that worship is more than the music we sing and play?

2. Read Temple's words and discuss what the important aspects of worship are that need renewed attention. "Worship is the submission of all our nature to God: to quicken the conscience by the holiness of God; To nourish the mind with the Truth of God; to purge the imagination by the beauty of God; to open up the heart to the love of God and to surrender the will to the purpose of God."[25]

3. Invite a few others to join together and prepare a worship gathering that includes the aspects of Eat, Pray, and Read together.

4. "Wouldn't it be wonderful for a coming generation to experience prayer as one of the most refreshing and renewing aspects of its corporate life?" What prayer experience could you prepare for your community to deepen the experience of prayer?

5. **Exercise:** Take a moment and write out a prayer of worship to the Lord that captures some of these truths. Declare the Lord's worth, praise His works, and renew your self-offering to Him.

Notes

[1] Wright, *Simply Christian: Why Christianity Makes Sense*, chap. 11.

[2] Bright, Bill. The Joy of Faithful Obedience: Your Way to God's Best. N.p.: David C. Cook, 2005. Print. 38

[3] (accessed March 21, 2014).

[4] Romans 12:1-2

[5] Piper: (accessed March 21, 2014).

[6] A statement from the Archbishop's committee on worship, 1905.

[7] Piper: (accessed March 21, 2014).

[8] Warren W. Wiersbe, *The Bible Exposition Commentary, vol. 1* (Wheaton, IL: Victor Books, 1996), 554.

[9] N. T. Wright, *Surprised by Hope: Rethinking Heaven, the Resurrection, and the Mission of the Church.*

[10] Written by Andy Park

[11] John R. W. Stott, source unknown

[12] For example, Hemmoraging Faith 2011 – found that nearly 70% of those raised in church in the 1990s had left church.

[13] These findings were results of my own non-scientific poll completed by invitation on Facebook Feb.2014

[14] Piper, , accessed March 21, 2014

[15] Milne, *The Message of John: Here Is Your King!*, 88–89.

[16] Stott, *The Message of Acts: The Spirit, the Church & the World*, 84–85.

[17] David Prior, *The Message of 1 Corinthians: Life in the Local Church*, *The Bible Speaks Today* (Leicester, England; Downers Grove, IL: InterVarsity Press, 1985), 190–191.

[18] R. C. Lucas, *Fullness & Freedom: The Message of Colossians & Philemon*, *The Bible Speaks Today* (Downers Grove, IL: InterVarsity Press, 1980), 173.

[19] Stott, *The Message of Acts: The Spirit, the Church & the World*, 82.

[20] Wright, *Simply Christian: Why Christianity Makes Sense*, 150.

[21] 1 Corinthians 11:24ff

[22] Stott, *The Message of Acts: The Spirit, the Church & the World*, 85–86.

[23] https://www.christianhistoryinstitute.org/incontext/article/augustine/

[24] Milne, *The Message of John: Here Is Your King!, 90.*

CHAPTER NINE

Zombie Churches and Vampire Christians!

"Since, then, you have been raised with Christ, set your hearts on things above, where Christ is, seated at the right hand of God. Set your minds on things above, not on earthly things. For you died, and your life is now hidden with Christ in God. When Christ, who is your life, appears, then you also will appear with him in glory"
(Col. 3:1-4 NIV).

ecently I read an article about the collapse of the real estate market in 2008 in the vicinity of Phoenix, Arizona. This collapse left the region with a vast number of unfinished neighborhoods that were apparently nicknamed "Zombie Subdivisions."[1] The article explains that these are communities that began with great hope and anticipation, but never became more than a shell of their promised reality. In many places, there are streets, sidewalks, driveways, partially completed homes, and even welcome signs, but there is no life, only abandoned projects that never reached completion.

It struck me that this could be an apt metaphor for the condition of some churches–they might be called "zombie churches!" Such churches show many of the outward signs of life: a building, worship services, weekly events, budget meetings, parking lots, and cool websites. However, a careful look reveals a genuine lack of (divine) life; it has been a long time since the life (development and promised transformation) that was hoped for has been seen in their midst.

Taking this illustration even further, part of the reason for the existence of "zombie churches" could be that they are filled with "vampire Christians!" Dallas Willard uses this phrase to refer to those who are not really interested in following Jesus; they simply "want some of His blood." Willard notes, "Some Christians today have come to believe that it is quite reasonable to be a 'vampire Christian.' In effect one says to Jesus, 'I'd like a little of your blood, please, but I don't care to be your student or have your character. In fact, won't you just excuse me while I get on with my life, and I'll see you in heaven.'"[2]

This vampire Christianity has led to a host of church attendees (if convenient) who are, to use the words of Kendra Creasy Dean, really only "Almost Christians."[3] The result leads to zombie churches, where the measurable qualities of character are little different than the Christ-less world around them.[4]

Rescue for the Zombies

Concern about the condition of the contemporary Western church has been met with a variety of proposed solutions. They focus on answers with various emphases such as ecclesiology (the church organization, "if we could just organize the way we approach leadership structures," etc.), pneumatology (the Holy Spirit, "the Holy Spirit is neglected and what we need is more miracles or supernatural events," etc.), missiology (the church's strategy for changing the world around it, whether that is through working for justice or caring for the environment, etc.), and secularizing culture (the reason for the current weakness in the church is that the culture has moved away from God, and it is no longer possible to have vibrant churches in this context) to name but a few of the solutions that have been a focus.

However, a more compelling diagnosis may be that the church has neglected its primary calling as expressed in what has been called the Great Commission of Jesus, found in Matthew 28:19ff, Acts 1:8, and Mark 16. It is tempting to quickly dismiss this challenge; after all, it could be offered that there is more preaching of the gospel in the world today than at any other time in history. How could the present malaise in parts of the church be a Great Commission issue? Consider again the words of Jesus in Matthew 28:18-20 (NIV):

"And Jesus came and said to them, "All authority in heaven and on earth has been given to me. Go therefore and make disciples of all nations, baptizing them in the name of the Father and of the Son and of the Holy Spirit, teaching them to observe all that I have commanded you. And behold, I am with you always, to the end of the age."

Jesus' primary call to action here is not going, teaching, and baptizing; it is *making disciples*. As Marshall and Payne write, "Sometimes our translations (of the Bible) give the impression that 'go' is the emphasis of the command, but the main verb of the sentence is 'make disciples,' with three subordinate principles hanging off it: going (or 'as your go'), baptizing, and teaching."[5]

There is no question that the church has been going, teaching, and baptizing, but have we attended to the central command of Jesus–that of making disciples? Again, there may well be a strong reaction by others that discipleship has been our primary focus in the church, and that certainly this cannot be the cause of the lackluster condition of the church today. The evidence offered for such a response might be, on the one hand, the various training programs that are offered on evangelism, biblical knowledge, or theology, as if this were the definition of being a disciple. On the other hand, others might point to the social action that the church is engaged in, to alleviate suffering and injustice in the name of Jesus, as if this were what it means to be a disciple. The question to ask is, "Are these the things that Jesus intended in telling His disciples to make disciples?"

> *The church has been going, teaching and baptizing, but have we attended to the central command of Jesus – that of making disciples?*

Michael Horton suggests that a key issue for today's church is its many diversions away from this main task of discipleship. He uses the military term "mission creep,"[6] defined as "the expansion of a project or mission beyond its original goals, often after initial successes," to expose the need for a renewed focus on the call to make disciples. Horton wants to "call us away from mission creep, centering our discipleship and our churches on the very specific sources, goals, strategies, and methods that Christ mandated for this time between his two comings,"[7] in particular to focus again on making disciples.

These words of Jesus, and indeed much of the New Testament, indicate that while discipleship may well include the outward actions of doing evangelism, growing in biblical knowledge, and engagement in social action, what we might call our *Deeds and Creeds*, discipleship has more to do with the personal transformation of the lives that are formed by obedience to Jesus. As the late philosopher and author on spiritual formation, Dallas Willard, writes, "Bible study, prayer, and church attendance, among the most commonly prescribed activities in Christian circles, generally have little effect for soul transformation."[8] What Jesus is saying in Matthew 28:20 is that He will always be present with His people, and the role of His disciples is to introduce others to Him and His way of life so that they too will experience His transforming presence.

This life-journey of being formed into the likeness of Jesus through the renewing power of the Holy Spirit and the practice of spiritual disciplines is what has been traditionally called spiritual formation. Dallas Willard gives this definition: "Spiritual formation in the Christian tradition is the process of increasingly being possessed and permeated by such character traits (of Jesus) as we walk in the easy yoke of discipleship with Jesus our teacher. From the inward character the deeds of love then naturally–but supernaturally—and transparently flow.... Our aim is to be pervasively possessed by Jesus through constant companionship with him. Like our brother Paul, 'this one thing I do;... I press on towards the goal!... that I might know Christ!'"[9]

If this is the right understanding of Jesus' command in Matthew 28, to make disciples, it then follows that spiritual formation is the ultimate aim of the Christian life when it is understood as the entire process of repentance, submission, and obedience to the Lord Jesus Christ. In fact, author James C. Wilhoit has written, "Spiritual formation is the task of the Church, period."[10] By this he does not mean it is the *only* task of the church; he affirms that the church needs to be committed to witness, worship, teaching, and compassion in the world, but these flow from lives that are increasingly being formed into the likeness of Christ.[11] It does need to be said that there are some forms of spiritual formation that have found a place in the church which are rooted in Eastern religions (New Age spirituality or humanism); these are not being advocated and need to be avoided.[12] If the practices being encouraged do not focus Christians on the person of Jesus and His finished work, we can be wary.

It might be asked, "Won't this emphasis on spiritual formation mean Christians will turn inward, focused on personal piety, and avoid reaching lost people with the gospel?" However, healthy spiritual formation is a call for all Christians to be constantly renewed in the gospel. "The gospel is the power of God for the beginning, middle, and end of salvation. It is not merely what we need to proclaim to unbelievers; the gospel also needs to permeate our entire Christian experience."[13] We can look at it this way: if Jesus were able to rub shoulders with more people in the world today, isn't it likely that many more of them would choose to follow Him? That is the intended effect of a greater focus on the spiritual formation leading to Christlikeness. As Michael Horton says, "The more we grow in this knowledge and experience of Christ, the more we are prepared to make a defense to anyone who asks you 'for the reason for the hope that is in you' and to do it with 'gentleness and respect' (1 Peter 3:15). Those who know what they believe and why they believe it, do not need to rely on memorized formulas. They do not need to be coaxed or browbeaten into sharing their faith. It becomes a natural part of everyday relationships and conversations."[14] We also need to remember that the content of the gospel is the person of Jesus (Mark 1:1), and when His presence is visible in us there is every likelihood that evangelism will happen. Living water is very appealing to thirsty people!

Silver Bullets: Defining a Process for Spiritual Formation

Despite well meaning promises and our own private hopes, the gospel is not a silver bullet that will instantly fix all of our character flaws and overcome all our fleshliness.[15] The gospel enables us to put off old ways of living and put on new ways of living, which will take effort on our part, but will be possible because of our new life in Christ. In Colossians 3:1-8, Paul reminds us of our new identity as Christians, raised to life with Christ, dead to the dominating power of sin, and hidden in Christ. Since this is true, he exhorts us to put to death the old ways of living. We may be drawn to the idea that something less than this death to self will produce transformation, but in fact it leaves us no further forward than before. Wilhoit critiques several contemporary approaches that promise spiritual formation or transformation but fall short of what Christ calls us to. Whether it is attending a conference, claiming certain biblical promises, or espousing certain author's teachings, all will fall short. "A Christian's deep Christlikeness will not be satisfied at the wells of products for spiritual growth but (only) with Christ (himself), the Living Water."[16] The call of Christ is to follow Him, to become His apprentices, to learn to walk in the life-giving rhythms of His grace.

"And calling the crowd to him with his disciples, he said to them, 'If anyone would come after me, let him deny himself and take up his cross and follow me. For whoever would save his life will lose it, but whoever loses his life for my sake and the gospel's will save it. For what does it profit a man to gain the whole world and forfeit his soul? For what can a man give in return for his soul? For whoever is ashamed of me and of my words in this adulterous and sinful generation, of him will the Son of Man also be ashamed when he comes in the glory of his Father with the holy angels'" (Mark 8:34-38).

To some of us this may seem to conflict with the truth of God's grace. However as Ephesians 2:8-10 shows us, grace means salvation cannot be earned, but it enables us to do the good works for which we are being formed. Dallas Willard quips, "Currently we are not only saved by grace; we are paralyzed by it."[17] In other words, our wonderful discovery of grace can liberate us from trying to earn God's love by our efforts. We may well then assume there is nothing that we can do at all, lest we be working (to earn God's favor); thus we may become stagnate, assuming there is nothing at all for us to do. Grace is the means not the end; it enables us to live lives pleasing to God, free from striving to earn His acceptance. Again Willard says, "Grace is not opposed to effort, it is opposed to earning. Earning is an attitude. Effort is an action.... In fact, nothing inspires and enhances effort like the experience of grace."[18]

> "Grace is not opposed to effort, it is opposed to earning." - Willard

We might depict the place of these habits and the process of spiritual formation as seen in the following diagram.

The spiritual formation process involves embracing new habits, which enable us to participate with Jesus in the formation of His character within us. In *Desiring the Kingdom*, Smith says, "Character is formed by the liturgy we participate in. Practices shape our habits, our habits shape our affections, which shape what we live for."[19]

These practices have traditionally been called "spiritual disciplines," and have been a normal part of the lives of those who follow Jesus. To be sure, various spiritual disciples have waxed and waned throughout the ages, at times due to neglect, and at other times due to the wrong emphases placed upon them. However, those who have grown in Christlikeness in every age are those who have chosen to embrace various disciplines as the means to draw near to Christ. Spiritual disciplines are habits that are developed to draw us near to God and allow us to hear Him on directions in life.

It might be asked, "Just what *are* spiritual disciplines?" They may not be the peculiar activities one first imagines. In fact, if you have been on the journey of following Christ very long, you will have already begun to discover some spiritual disciplines and may be encouraged by being introduced to others.

> Spiritual Discipline: A habit in life that brings you back to God, and opens you to His directions in life.

A partial list would include spiritual habits such as:

- Solitude—Learning to be alone in the presence of the Lord.
- Silence—Learning to listen to the voice of the Spirit.
- Fasting—Giving priority to spiritual appetites over physical ones.
- Sabbath—Giving special time to God in the week.
- Serving—Learning to prefer others in the name of Christ.
- Submission—Recognizing the sovereignty of God in placing others over us.
- Worship—Giving God His due praises in all seasons of life.
- Prayer—Speaking to the Lord and listening for His voice.
- Bible reading—Discovering God's truth, learning about His will.
- Accountability—Accepting the help of God's family to live like His child.

- Giving—Overcoming the power of greed and self-centeredness.

When we look at Jesus in the Gospels, we see that He had a life of rhythm. He was not always preaching or doing miracles, there were times of quiet, prayer, fasting, fellowship, reflection, etc. Those who desire to follow Him and experience His transforming power will need to embrace His lifestyle too.

"And immediately He made His disciples get into the boat and go ahead of Him to the other side to Bethsaida, while He Himself was sending the multitude away. And after bidding them farewell, *he departed to the mountain to pray*" (Mark 6:45-46).

In fact, the scriptures even imply that although He was the eternally perfect Son of God, Jesus needed spiritual formation to complete His calling on earth. For example, He had never before needed to overcome temptation, but His incarnation would require this. His practice of spiritual disciplines brought about that formation and thus His life to completion.

"And being found in human form, he humbled himself by becoming obedient to the point of death, even death on a cross" (Phil. 2:8).

"Although he was a son, he learned obedience through what he suffered. And being made perfect, he became the source of eternal salvation to all who obey him" (Heb. 5:8-9).

As the scholar Raymond Brown says, "It is important for us to see that when Jesus surrendered himself entirely to God's will, he obeyed not only in order to honor God but also to help us to see what obedience is all about. In his exposition of this passage, Calvin says: 'He did this for our benefit, to give us the instance and the pattern of His own submission.... If we want the obedience of Christ to be of advantage to us, we must copy it.'"[20]

While this topic can take us through a theological minefield, the main idea is that Jesus, our Lord, modeled spiritual disciplines and, He invites us to do the same. Once again, these are not undertaken to earn God's favor, but are part of the favored-family lifestyle that enable us to have greater enjoyment of the Father's presence and power (Matt. 6:33).

Perhaps a useful analogy would be a young promising athlete who cannot afford to join an elite club team, but who is noticed by a generous benefactor. The athlete is given a sponsorship to be a part of the team as an act of grace. Now as a part of the team, the athlete will undertake the training regimens in order to be able to function as a part of the team. All analogies fail at some point; however, God invites us by grace to become a part of His family, we then embrace those habits which will enable us to fully enjoy that family membership and the heart of the Father.

COMMUNITAS: Light That Raises Zombies!

There is a way to raise those wandering zombies to life again, by filling them with the brilliant light of Christ. We need each a context that encourages us to embrace and enjoy spiritual disciplines – that is meant to be the church. The apostle Paul urges the church to press onward together in community so that their lives will pour forth light into the dark world around them. (Remind yourself that the "you" in these verses is plural – i.e. ya'll as they say in the American South.)

"Therefore, my beloved, as you have always obeyed, so now...work out your own salvation with fear and trembling, for it is God who works in you, both to will and to work for his good pleasure. Do all things without grumbling or disputing, that you may be blameless and innocent, children of God without blemish in the midst of a crooked and twisted generation, among whom you shine as lights in the world" (Phil. 2:12-15).

Three Comments on Communitas and Life-Giving Light

1. We need His family for spiritual formation. Paul is calling the whole community to be those who will work out what God has worked into them by grace. The "you" and "your" (Phil. 2:12) in the original text are plural words, e.g. "all of you" work at this together. This is the place where encouragement, support, and accountability strengthen the work of His transforming presence. "The community is to encourage us when we falter, strengthen us to turn to Christ in our weakness, and challenge us to finish well. The fertile field for formation is in a community genuinely aware of the depth of their sin and the reality of their spiritual thirst."[21]

B.E.L.L.S: A Model for Communal Spiritual Disciplines:

The Australian pastor and theologian, Michael Frost, tells of how his church community has sought to engage in spiritual disciplines in the realm of daily life. Together they seek to engage in and encourage one another in specific behaviors that both form themselves spiritually and further their commitment to missional living. They use the acronym B.E.L.L.S. to clarify specific disciplines, which they prioritize during the week. Imagine how embracing a simple pattern of habits like this might transform your church.[22]

Ring the B.E.L.L.S. together:

BLESSING— The Hebrew word for "blessing" (*barak*) means "to empower to strength." We seek God's blessing and pass that blessing on to others. *Bless one person this week (preferably a non-Christ follower).*

EATING— Sharing food has always been central to a life of community. We want to place worship and communion back where it began, as a provider's delight in the middle of the shared table. *Eat with one person this week (preferably a non-Christ follower).*

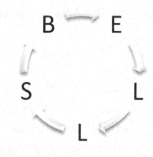

LISTENING— We believe that God is capable of speaking to us. We do not confine Him to any particular medium, but we try to be attentive to His voice, wherever and whenever it speaks. *Take time to listen to God for one hour/week (listening, not talking).*

LEARN— We desire to take on the image of God and to participate in His plan. We seek out knowledge about God to help us to do this. *Study Jesus' life a little bit each week from the Gospels. How did He live? With whom did He interact? What were His commands? Then "go" live like Jesus did.*

SENT— We are ambassadors who bear God's image in the world. Remind yourselves regularly that we are "sent" to participate in God's activity and mission in the world. *Take time each day to reflect on the question: "How have I worked with or resisted Jesus today?"*

2.   **We need His presence.** The safeguard against becoming another wandering zombie or legalistic cult is the reminder that "it is God who works in you, both to will and to

work..." (Phil. 2:13). The community can engage in spiritual disciplines together, not as emblems of personal piety, but as shared longings for the formation of Christ in them. "Genuine spiritual formation requires that the community deeply understands that they cannot cure the sickness of their souls through willpower alone."[23] They remind one another that the gospel is for the beginning, middle, and end of the Christian life; it is the continuing work of God's mercy in us.

3. We need to press onward. The persistence of obedience will involve effort on the part of the church community. Again, not to earn God's favor, but as those who know it personally. Paul reminds the church of their imputed identity, "children of God without blemish..." (Phil. 2:15). In spiritual formation we are not orphans left alone to figure these things out, we have His body the Church, both locally and universally, to support us in the endeavor. "Christian spiritual formation: (1) is intentional; (2) is communal; (3) requires our engagement; (4) is accomplished by the Holy Spirit; (5) is for the glory of God and the service of others; and (6) has as its means and end the imitation of Christ."[24]

CONCLUSION

The hope for the world is the Lord Jesus Christ and His all-encompassing and completed work at Calvary. The challenge to the Church is to heed the call to become those who, through grace, will be formed and transformed by Him. Our world needs to see authentic disciples who are obediently making disciples. Dallas Willard summarizes, "Who can show them the way if the people identified with the cause of Christ in this world are not prepared to teach and exemplify a process of spiritual formation that will result in an outflow of Christ from their

> "Christian spiritual formation is simply indispensable" – Dallas Willard

deepest heart and character...from the viewpoint of those responsible to lead in Christ's program of making students from all ethnic groupings, immersing them in the reality of the triune name and teaching them to do all things he has commanded us (Matt. 28:19-20), Christian spiritual formation is simply indispensable."[25]

Discussion Questions

1. Discuss the idea of spiritual formation as the answer to many of the weaknesses evident in the church.

2. What are some examples of spiritual disciplines that are seen in the life of Jesus?

3. What are some examples of spiritual disciplines that have been helpful to you, and what has been challenging in this area?

4. What might it look like for your church to engage more intentionally in a process of spiritual formation?

5. Try the actions of Michael Frost's B.E.L.L.S. (mentioned above) for an agreed period of time with a group of others and discuss the results.

Notes

[1] (Accessed July 24, 2013).

[2] Willard, *The Great Omission*, 14.

[3] Dean, *Almost Christian*.

[4] (accessed July 25, 2013) "Notional Christians - adults who say they are Christian but have never made a profession of faith in Jesus Christ - represent almost half of all people attending Christian churches in the U.S. In total, they are about one-third of the adult population. These individuals were more likely to behave in ways that characterized non-Christians than to reflect the behavior of born again adults. In other words, their faith does not seem to be a defining factor in many of their lifestyle choices."

[5] Marshall, *The Trellis and the Vine*, 12.

[6] The term was first used regarding the U. N. Mission in Somalia in the early 1990s.

[7] Horton, *The Gospel Commission*, 8.

[8] Dallas Willard, *The Great Omission: Rediscovering Jesus' Essential Teachings on Discipleship* (San Francisco: Harper, 2006).

[9] Willard, *The Great Omission*, 16.

[10] Wilhoit, *Spiritual Formation as If the Church Mattered*, 15. He defines Spiritual formation: "Christian spiritual formation refers to the intentional communal process of growing in our relationship with God and becoming conformed to Christ through the power of the Holy Spirit," (23).

[11] Willard, *The Great Omission*, 48ff, 112ff. See further in *The Great Omission*; Willard offers fuller treatment of other non-Christian forms of spiritual formation.

[12] Willard, *The Great Omission*.

[13] Wilhoit, *Spiritual Formation as If the Church Mattered*, 29.

[14] Horton, *The Gospel Commission*.

[15] 2 Corinthians 5:17 does assure those who are reconciled to God through Christ that they have a new blameless position before God, but 5:4 reminds of the process of our condition being changed in this life.

[16] Wilhoit, *Spiritual Formation As If the Church Mattered*, 51–54.

[17] Willard, *The Great Omission*, 166.

[18] Ibid., 61, 80.

[19] Smith, *Desiring the Kingdom*.

[20] Raymond Brown, *The Message of Hebrews: Christ Above All*, *The Bible Speaks Today* (Leicester, England; Downers Grove, IL: InterVarsity Press, 1988), 102.

[21] Wilhoit, *Spiritual Formation as If the Church Mattered*, 63.

[22] Frost, *Exiles*.

[23] Ibid., 63.

[24] Ibid., 27.

[25] Willard, *The Great Omission*, 120ff.

CHAPTER TEN

Future Church

"Jesus replied, 'Blessed are you, Simon son of Jonah, for this was not revealed to you by flesh and blood, but by my Father in heaven. And I tell you that you are Peter, and on this rock I will build my church, and the gates of Hades will not overcome it'" (Matt. 16:17-18 NIV).

Surprisingly in spite of what one might expect, there is very little recorded of Jesus speaking about the church in the gospels. In fact, there are only two recorded instances in the four gospels where this word is found on His lips. This does not mean however, that the church was a later invention or a non-priority. The priority of God throughout the ages has been to create a new family who can know Him and His eternal purposes.[1] In this passage, Jesus is on a personal retreat with His disciples in the northerly town of Caesarea, named in honor of Caesar, emperor of the Roman Empire. This town was also the home of a great imposing temple dedicated to the worship of Caesar and the multitude of pagan gods that were embraced in civic religion. Against this backdrop, Jesus asks His followers who they understood Him to be and Peter rightly replies, "You are the Son of God." This conclusion by Peter was the result of many events and consistent explanations from Jesus over the past three years together. "Simon Peter comes to recognize who this carpenter-teacher really is. No category of human exaltation can embrace him. He surpasses them all. Here Peter is the spokesman for the conclusion to which he, and the band of disciples, had been driven by all they had experienced; Jesus is the Messiah, *the Son of the living God.*"[2] The earliest recipients of the gospels would not have missed that this was the title (Son of God) and allegiance reserved for the Roman Emperor alone, ascribing it to another was treasonous and could lead to death. Therefore, to call Jesus the Lord and Son of God was no insignificant religious impulse.

Jesus links *this* correct understanding of His identity with the global movement that would result from His coming into the world, His Church. The Church would be a new people gathered by Him, enabled through the events of His crucifixion and resurrection, and enabled by the Holy Spirit to live in His mission in the world. "The Messiah was always seen (in Jewish understanding) *with his people.* He was not going to be a solitary phenomenon. He would be the head of the renewed Israel. He would be accompanied by his *qāhāl*, his congregation, those who acknowledged him. Nothing could be more natural than the mention here of the Messiah's people just after he has been plainly hailed as the Messiah."[3] As the centuries have unfolded, Christ's words have proven true, He *has* "built His church" and today it encompasses more than 2.5 billion people on the planet. It is no trivial Jewish sect; His Church continues to grow with peoples from every "tribe and tongue" as John prophesied that it would be. Despite centuries of persecutions, cultural barriers, language barriers, hostility to its message, the Church of Jesus has grown and continues Jesus' mission, even though imperfectly.

However, while it is wonderful to see the work of Jesus the master builder and the global progress of the church, the picture of the advance in recent years in North America is less encouraging, and in fact, quite disturbing. Some have said that unless there is a dramatic change in the present trajectory of the church, its future in the West is very bleak. While the church is growing at rates unknown in history in many new contexts such as in India, China, and many parts of Africa, it is in rapid decline in many parts of North America and Europe. The future is in the hands of the Lord who promised He would build His Church, but it is still important to know some of the realities of the present course of the church in North America.

In 2010, Haiti was devastated by an earthquake in its overcrowded capital city, Port au Prince, which led to catastrophic loss of life. It is estimated that two-thirds of the buildings collapsed and some 250,000 people were killed. One Haitian leader, surveying the destruction, focused on the schools and universities, which were destroyed. He said, "Because the earthquake struck in the afternoon a lot of schools and universities were filled with students; the losses of these young people were great... The loss of the national treasure of an entire generation of Haiti's best and brightest is a loss that cannot be measured or replaced."4

> "The loss of ... entire generation ... is a loss that cannot be measured or replaced."

Surveying the data of trends in the North American church reveals another alarming generational loss in our midst. This development is the loss of vast numbers of those who were raised in churches over the past two decades. Research conducted in the U.S. and Canada reveal a staggering loss of most of the generation known as the Millennials. In one study titled "Hemorrhaging Faith," the authors write, "this research project is about taking faith decay as seriously as our culture takes physical disease. (This is) sobering new research on Canadian 'raised Christian' 18 to 34 year-olds. For every five Catholic and Mainline Protestant kids who attended church at least weekly in the 1980s and '90s only one still attends at least weekly now as an adult; for those raised in Evangelical traditions it is one in two. *And that's not all. Most who have quit attending altogether also have dropped their Christian affiliation"* (emphasis mine). The picture is much the same in the U.S. In 2006, the Barna group raised an alarm with American data suggesting six in ten churchgoing teens become spiritually disengaged after high school. 60% of 'Churched Millennials' are now de-churched. Looking at similar numbers in the British context, one researcher[5] quipped, "you had a better chance of survival on the

> 60% of 'Churched Millennials' are now de-churched.

Titanic than a child's faith has in our churches: 1523 out of 2228 passengers and crew were drowned during the sinking of the Titanic – a loss of 68%. But, according to research, of every class of 10 one to nine-year-olds in Sunday School in 1985, only three were still connected with the church in 2005, a loss of 70%!"

Who are Millennials and What are Some Distinctives?

The Millennials were born between 1980-2004;[6] they have been variously called: "GEN Y," 20-Somethings, Generation Next, The Me-Gen, Screen-agers, Trophy Kids, and the Peter Pan generation because of their delayed adulthood.[7] It is important to resist stereotyping such a large group because, as one researcher reminds, "defining a generation can be challenging, as the term can have several different meanings. In general, a generation is a group of individuals who are about the same age and have experienced, most often as children or young adults, specific historical events, such as an economic crisis, an economic boom, a war, or significant political changes. These events may influence their views of the world."[8]

There are some interesting details to note about this generation.[9] Millennials are the largest generation in American history, some 95 million compared to just 78 million Baby Boomers. The same is true in Canada where they are at least as large a number (9 million) as the Boomer generation.[10] By 2020, nearly 50 percent of the U.S. workforce will consist of Millennials; in Canada, the forecasts are 75 percent by the year 2028. They are the most ethnically diverse generation in history due to high global immigration rates. Millennials are highly concerned about social justice issues and environmentalism.

They are "Digital natives":[11]a creative and resilient, data-saturated, wired-gen raised with immediate access to information. Millennials are the most educated generation in history, according to Pew Research, with a higher percentage attending college than ever before (78%). Millennials are concerned for significance vs. success: Millennials have less desire to end up like Gordon Gecko or Bud Fox, the greedy heroes from Wall Street, and more likely to emulate Blake Mycoskie, the founder of *TOMS* shoes. Many now seek life mentoring about how to apply their knowledge and develop their relational intelligence.

Millennials were raised with history's highest rate of parental dislocation; more experienced divorce and alternative home-life. A significant percentage of them grew up in divorced and separated homes and have had to navigate parenting deficits.

Millennials are the least religious generation in history. They have a new category of identity in religious studies, "Spiritual But Not Religious" (SBNR). They may say that they are spiritual, but only a small fraction of them say that is important in their lives. The sad reality is that most Millennials don't think about religion at all.

Pressures on Millennial Faith

Many have asked, "Why is there an exodus of Millennials from the church?" The answer to the question is complex, but it would include a combination of the following factors. **Post-modern culture** is a reaction to the concern of being controlled by the power claims of others. The result of this cultural influence is the rejection of all claims to absolute truth, which are deemed to be coercive, and instead all truth is to be personally determined (apparently that truth is absolute). Therefore, "if truth is at best personal and all truths are equally valid, how can anyone claim that Christianity is uniquely true?"

Coupled with post-modernism is a **lost confidence in authority.** Millennials have experienced colossal failures of leaders both within the church and in the wider culture leading to great distrust of authority. The failures have included most aspects of life such as academics who faked their research, and investors who deceived and bilked millions of dollars from trusting clients. Moreover, there have been countless religious leaders who have abused their flock for selfish gain and athletes who have cheated and lied to win. While it is true that every generation has had flawed heroes, theirs has had a greater number and from every part of the spectrum. As a result, as Kinnaman from Barna says: "Millennials are rethinking most of the institutions that arbitrate life, from marriage and media, to government and church."[12]

Rabbit Ears to Cable

Another factor that has been part of the Millennial exodus is the onslaught of **worldview challenges.** In forty years we have moved from rabbit-ears to cable T.V. A generation ago the television was limited to two or three stations, and a limited number of shows dominated the culture. Most people knew the characters of MASH or Bonanza because the viewing competition was limited. Today, with hundreds of channels available online or cable, the array of shows is staggering, and committed audiences are much smaller. Kendra Creasy Dean, author of *Almost Christian*, notes that many church leaders and parents grew up in a culture where there were only a few worldview options, and the dominant worldview of the culture was Christianity. It was the big story that most in the culture were at least familiar with. Millennials have grown up in a world with hundreds of competing stories, or channels to choose from so to speak. They have been forced to the bedrock of conviction to discern what is really true. Again as David Kinnamon writes, "It's hard to know how to live with the onslaught of information, worldviews and options they are faced with every day. One of the specific criticisms young adults frequently make about Christianity is that it does not offer deep, thoughtful or challenging answers to life in a complex culture."[13] The church needs to learn afresh how to convey the powerful reasons for faith in Christ. Just turning the volume up does not give more clarity. There is a need in the church for renewed apologetics in a context where the Christian story is not the loudest or dominant voice. Millennials need to hear why it makes sense to trust Christ, how He is unique, and why it matters to gather with His people.

Additional to the cultural shifts and effects, there has also been the issue of **changes in home life**. The church has not been immune from the collapse of marriage and even definitions of family. These shifts and changes have had a major impact on the lives of this generation raised in church. The authors of "Hemorrhaging Faith" comment, "tumult in parental marriage is a significant factor in kids leaving church... Study after study indicates that parents are usually the most significant spiritual influence in their teen's lives. It is reasonable, then, to expect that changes to parents' marital status or their rate of attendance would influence the spiritual lives of their children."[14]

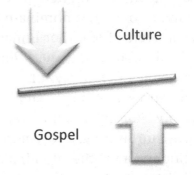

Culture

Gospel

One final piece of the puzzle to consider about why Millennials have left the church would be the way in which **church has failed to accomplish its mission.** It has been said that mission involves "engaging the ever-changing **culture** with the never-changing **gospel.**"[15] On the human side of things, there is a two-fold task if the church is going to succeed in mission: understanding the depth and wonder of God's good news, and understanding the depth and complexity of the culture in which it is proclaimed. The failure to do this well has certainly had an impact on the spiritual development of Millennials. The question is which of these two mission priorities has been neglected most?

On one hand, some feel the exodus has primarily to do with the church's **failure to navigate the changing culture** and provide a meaningful context to grow in spiritually. For example, David Kinnaman, President of BARNA Research, suggests in his book *You Lost Me!* that the exodus is the result of the church being fearful, anti-science, controlling, and hostile to culture. The solutions he suggests are to adjust ways of doing church that are more engaging with culture. This would include more interaction around the challenging questions of life, technology, ethics, and the ways in which scripture speaks to these issues. This is certainly a valid observation; there are many complex issues around us, and there is a need to have candid and clear conversations in order to gain confidence in the hope we have. However, this type of engagement must be an authentic approach to clarity and not just an effort to keep young adults in church. Listen to Millennial author Rachel Evans:

"Time and again, the assumption among Christian leaders, and evangelical leaders in particular, is that the key to drawing twenty-something's back to church is simply to make a few style updates–edgier music, more casual services, a coffee shop in the fellowship hall, a pastor who wears skinny jeans, an updated website that includes online giving. But here's the thing: Having been advertised to our whole lives, we Millennials have highly sensitive BS meters, and we're not easily impressed with consumerism or performances."[16]

Others suggest it has been less to do with the failure to engage culture adequately and more to do with the church's failure to **communicate the never-changing Gospel adequately.** One commentator summarized it this way: The church didn't "lose" the Millennials at all; they were simply never actually *in* church to begin with. (Meaning "in the church" in the biblical sense of belonging through spiritual new birth and transformation.) No doubt many have been in church buildings and programs, but they have had little exposure to Christ-centered discipleship. Ed Stetzer commented on the teaching that this generation received saying, "Too many youth ministries were simply holding tanks with pizza, even though youth desired a faith that transformed their lives and the world."[17] In the words of a Millennial Blogger, "Ben": "Our serious questions, if they were answered at all, were often answered with simple platitudes and insufficient clichés. We weren't taught the Bible. The last generation was good at proof-

> "Too many youth ministries were simply holding tanks with pizza…" - Stetzer

texting, but failed to demonstrate that the whole of God's Word was 'living and active, sharper than any two-edged sword' (Heb. 4:12). My generation, as a result, has very limited Bible knowledge."[18]

After extensive research on Millennials and faith, sociologist Christian Smith suggested that the *de facto* dominant faith among American Christian youth was what he has called "moralistic, therapeutic deism."[19] This term is the distillation of what young Christians told researchers it meant to be a

> "moralistic, therapeutic, deism."
>
> – Christian Smith

Christian. Christianity for them in essence is defined this way, "God wants you to keep rules, He wants you to feel good about yourself, and yet realistically God is not personally involved with us"! The researchers were shocked to hear little mention of the person of Jesus and almost no reference to Christian beliefs such as might be found in the Apostles' Creed, for example.

Kendra Creasy Dean, author of *Almost Christian*, writes, "The problem does not seem to be that churches are teaching young people badly, but that we are doing an exceedingly good job of teaching youth what we really believe, namely, that Christianity is not a big deal, that God requires little, and the church is a helpful social institution filled with nice people...." She goes on to say that "If churches practice moralistic, therapeutic deism in the name of Christianity, then getting teenagers to church more often is not the solution (conceivably it could make things worse)."

The reason some Millennials are not in church is a genuine spiritual hunger that is continually met with religious junk food. *"You can't hand us a latte and then go about business as usual and expect us to stick around. We're not leaving the church* *because we don't find the cool factor there; we're leaving the church **because we don't find Jesus there!**"[20]* In the words of the authors of the "Hemorrhaging Faith" research project, "For significant numbers of youth and young adults, churches are not places where they expect to experience the love of God and answered prayer."

Future Engagement

After sharing some of these findings about the Millennial Exodus at a conference, a church leader spoke up and asked the obvious question. "We can see these things are true, but what can we do to change the course of this situation in our churches?" Our answer has to begin with seeking God together in prayer, confessing our failures, and asking the Lord of the Church to guide us. Added to genuine seeking of our Lord, we can change some of our objectives and make the following objectives greater priorities: creating an open culture in church, greater expectancy in worship gatherings, and striving for a more holistic model of church life.

Authentic and Open Culture in Church

Some Millennials have disengaged from their churches because it appears to them that they do not have a welcome voice, few places of significance to serve, and an unwelcome place to ask genuine questions that need answers. An important step to take would be an honest admission in our churches that we have lost them unintentionally and need them to help us navigate back to a place that is both authentic to scripture and welcoming to the emerging generation. As Rachel Evans has said, "But I would encourage church leaders eager to win Millennials back to sit down and really talk with them about what they're looking for and what they would like to contribute to a faith community.... Ask them 'If you could help change something in

God's world what would it be? How could you tackle it? What could we do to help you?'"[21]

This is not a call to cater to every whim and desire of those who are not interested in biblical discipleship, as sometimes may have happened in the "seeker" focus of past decades. Instead, it is an invitation to work together on the mission of Christ in our world, and to admit that we have missed vital aspects of reaching a younger generation. As churches reach the stabilized part of their life cycle, the focus can often move away from crucial questions and struggles of those who are new to faith or still exploring.

I recently spoke at a University Christian Fellowship retreat and offered an open session to discuss questions that students might have. It was eye opening to hear what they are confronted with and how they desire biblical answers for many of the issues they face, and how they feel little help in their local church contexts. Many of them wanted to know what answers could be found about Jesus and gay culture. Too often challenging issues like this are unwelcomed topics.

Another aspect of creating an open and authentic culture in church is to be honest about dealing with disappointments. Too often our preaching and teaching convey dishonest and unbiblical truths about the realities of the Christ life. We need to share our own experiences of disappointments and heartache in many areas, including:

1. Others in church – let them see that we love Jesus and His church even when there is ugliness. These encounters often come as a stunning surprise and leave young and older Christians broken by the wayside.

2. Themselves – they will fail, and they need to see how we can come back when we fall. As leaders, we need to share

how the gospel has helped us deal with the personal failures we have had.

3. God – Young people need a solid faith that helps them to know how to face hard knocks when they come. Can we say, "Though the fig tree should not blossom...yet I will rejoice in the LORD..." (Hab. 3:17-18)?

This was a key finding in the "Hemorrhaging Faith" study, the authors noted. "Young adults would rather their parents be vulnerably honest about their spiritual walk (including the stumbles) than falsely pious or disengaged about the subject altogether."[22]

This open and authentic culture can be developed by working together, perhaps inviting a group of those who are disengaged to join with some leaders in a working group to answer some key questions. These could include; What kind of setting could we establish to explore questions together? What are the things that make it awkward to invite non-Christians to church? What issues do we need to teach about? What are you hearing from God? Are there ways we can hear God together? What do you think the Lord wants us to address in our community? The discoveries made through such a process of open discussion and exploration with an emerging generation of young believers could completely change the course of a generation. However, there is another area that needs consideration about the kind of gatherings we are a part of.

Expectancy in Worship

Again the prophetic voice from a past generation, A. W. Tozer, once said that if God were to remove the Holy Spirit from our churches, 90 percent of our activities would carry on and, we would never notice the difference. An honest admission by many of us is that we have long lost any great sense of expectancy in worship, the anticipation that God may speak, act, move, etc. Often this is because we have settled for well-worn patterns of worship that have become second nature to us. Lest we assume this is only true of certain Christian traditions, we need to remember that all churches have liturgical styles of worship; it is the pattern we follow when we gather to worship. This can become dull and rote or vibrant and engaging. What matters is the perspective that we have. Have we settled for our culture's latest offering of what appeals to us, or have we determined to make our gatherings a place where we seek eagerly after the Lord?

Len Sweet has written about worship that is EPIC, in which he offers an acrostic to enable us to remember important values in worship. These are good corrections to some of what has become the norm in churches having been influenced by a seeker culture. These are contrasted in the diagram below with what we might call a "seeking culture." We gather to seek the living God who has first sought us, not as disengaged consumers viewing an offering, but as those who eagerly desire to meet with and hear from God.

Too often we have settled for worship gatherings that are entirely predictable offerings of information that is personally pietistic and easily kept in the confines of an unused notebook. Imagine, instead, a gathering that invites all participants to experience both community and the transcendence of God through the thoughtful use of guided worship and exercises aided by imagery that moves us toward God.

An example that I have used in communicating on these issues in a seminar context is to prepare the space ahead of time. As participants arrive, there is worship music playing, lower lighting, a cross, and perhaps a candle. I invite those coming in to reflect on the worship music and join in if they like. As they view the cross, they are guided to pray for others in their lives that need to know the love of God in a fresh way. After a few moments, they are also invited to move to a poster on a wall and write names of those needing God's touch as a tangible way to express prayers. There are many ways to direct a worship gathering, this is just one, but it incorporates the values of EPIC worship and for many, this has helped greatly.

'EPIC WORSHIP'		
What is meant	Seeker	Seeking
E	Entertaining	Experiential
P	Presentation	Participatory
I	Individualistic	Image-rich
C	Conceptual	Communal

A Holistic Model of Church

Let's consider one last area as a part of this chapter on Future Church: to seek to refocus our image on defining the aspects of the life of a holistic church. When all participants have a complete image of what it is we are part of, it makes the serving we offer and sacrifices we make more intelligible.

For the church to function in its full dimensional strength we need a model that includes the whole Bible, whole world, whole church, and whole gospel; each of these will be expanded upon below. 23

WHOLE GOSPEL: SPIRITUAL FORMATION

The Bible is more than a four-page pamphlet with pictures, and its message is a rich narrative that encompasses all of life.

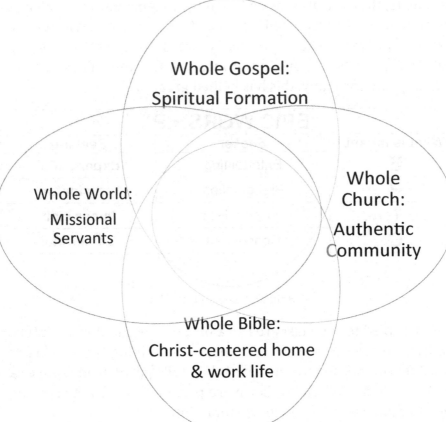

For the church to be a healthy community in the world, we need the whole Bible, not just a few favorite passages. Holistic churches know that the gospel involves more than mentally accepting a simple set of concepts in order to get into heaven someday. Sadly, this is what the gospel message is often reduced to in our culture and the result has been disastrous for the church. The call of Christ to everyone is God's gracious offer of new life through the completed offering of Christ on the cross. It is also the gift of a new power for living through His resurrected life. However, the acceptance of Christ's offer will be evidenced in willing obedience and complete submission to the life changing work of Jesus who desires to change us.[24] As Dietrich Bonhoeffer said, "When Christ calls a person, He calls them to come and die."[25] That dying to self and to the world sort of obedience is what has historically been called discipleship or spiritual formation. By which is meant, "the grace-directed process of growth into Christlikeness, that involves the renewing of the mind, heart and habits, through God's word and God's presence, which is the expected norm of Historic Christianity."[26]

In a church age that has largely lost sight of this reality of the Christian life, the call to such a life appears almost nonsensical. However, this is the call of Christ that He summons us to,[27] not one of temporary health and wealth and happy marriages in this world, but a transformed life by laboring and cooperating with the Holy Spirit to form a new nature within us. It is what N. T. Wright, in his book *After You Believe: Why Christian Character Matters*, calls the "hard-fought new nature."[28] This is not seeking to be justified by works, but working with the one who has justified us, to see His character formed within us, and our old nature put to death (Col. 3:1-8). Once again, hear the words of Bonhoeffer with echoing clarity, "When all is said and done, the life of faith is nothing if not an unending struggle of the spirit with every available weapon against the flesh."[29] A renewed commitment to the whole Bible will include a process for spiritual formation that is clear to all in the church. All are invited and shown how to proceed in the journey of following Christ together. There will be honest admission in our church life

> "...the life of faith is nothing if not an unending struggle of the spirit with every available weapon against the flesh."

of the trials and pitfalls, as well as celebrations of the advances that God has made in our lives.

We may well discover that spiritual formation or authentic discipleship has not been rejected by an emerging generation, but that the lack of it has turned them away. As Thom Rainer remarks from his research on Millennials, "This generation is doctrinally serious. At least the Christians among the Millennials care deeply about doctrine. More and more Millennial Christians will be in churches that are deeper in doctrine both from the preaching and within the groups of the church."[30] As leaders take seriously the health of the future church they can gain confidence that there is a desire for a robust faith in this generation. At the same time, we need the humility to admit that not all we have espoused is an example of that. Again, words from the "Hemorrhaging Faith" study:

"We must repent of transmitting a consumerist 'easy road' understanding of the gospel and seek instead through mentoring and an emphasis on prayer to involve youth and young adults in God's story as it has been told through the ages. Practices such as lectio divina (in which the steps are to read, meditate, pray and contemplate) may reveal aspects of Scripture that would be less obvious through a more rigid approach."[31]

WHOLE CHURCH: AUTHENTIC COMMUNITY

Jesus' words to the disciples on the night before His crucifixion are a haunting reminder of what He says is the genuine evidence that we are really His people. "By this all people will know that you are my disciples, if you have love for one another" (John 13:35). Another aspect of being a holistic church that is compelling, authentic and engaging is that, at its core, it is a caring community. This is what can be seen in the earliest pages of the book of Acts and continues in the brightest periods of history. In his remarkable book, *The Rise of Christianity: How the Obscure, Marginal Jesus Movement Became the Dominant Religious Force in the Western World in a Few Centuries*, Rodney Stark analyzes the remarkable birth and growth of the Christian movement against all odds. One of the factors he highlights is the remarkable community that was undeniable to a watching pagan world.

" . . . Christianity served as a revitalization movement that arose in response to the misery, chaos, fear, and brutality of life in the urban Greco-Roman world. . . . Christianity revitalized life in Greco-Roman cities by providing new norms and new kinds of social relationships able to cope with many urgent problems. To cities filled with the homeless and impoverished, Christianity offered charity as well as hope. To cities filled with newcomers and strangers, Christianity offered an immediate basis for attachment. To cities filled with orphans and widows, Christianity provided a new and expanded sense of family. To cities torn by violent ethnic strife, Christianity offered a new basis for social solidarity. And to cities faced with epidemics, fire, and earthquakes, Christianity offered effective nursing services. . . . *For what they brought was not simply an urban movement, but a new culture capable of making life in Greco-Roman cities more tolerable*"[32] (emphasis added).

The future of the Church is not rooted in the hip and hot fads of the present culture. Rather, it is rooted in the ancient convention that marks the early church of doing life together, and of sharing and encouraging one another in the power of Christ. The lack of this experience is one factor that has caused many young adults to leave and search for an alternate community. There is a finding verified by current research: "Youth and young adults who are not engaged in the church have not experienced a sense of belonging and community in their church contexts."[33] In fact, the social dislocation that many of this generation have experienced has made them especially attuned to seek authentic community. "They will only go to churches where they can easily connect with others. Unlike the Boomers, they refuse to be worship-only attendees. They desire to be in more relational settings. Churches with healthy groups will be very attractive to Millennials."[34]

Once again, the research that explores why so many Millennials have left the church found this absence of significant relationships in the church to be a major factor. As the Barna group noted, 60 percent of those who stayed in churches have a mentoring relationship with an older person, while 90 percent who left did not. Mentoring does not need to be a complicated and structured relationship; it simply involves living life openly through the various stages of life. Holistic churches must recapture the value of being a community where it is possible to model how to:

- Experience God's love and care.
- Experience answered prayer and guidance.
- See the redemptive power of God in our relationships and learn to forgive.
- Ask and discuss difficult questions about faith and Christian ethics.
- Understand the gospel at a deep level.

WHOLE WORLD: MISSIONAL SERVANTHOOD

Our wired world has brought information overload[35] into our lives and with it an immediate sense of the injustice of life for many on the planet. Jesus declares that His mandate as the Suffering Servant of Isaiah was to address the cause of injustice and ultimately bring about God's justice.

"And the scroll of the prophet Isaiah was given to him. He unrolled the scroll and found the place where it was written,

'The Spirit of the Lord is upon me,
because he has anointed me
to proclaim good news to the poor.
He has sent me to proclaim liberty to the captives
and recovering of sight to the blind,
to set at liberty those who are oppressed,
to proclaim the year of the Lord's favor'" (Luke 4:17-19, NIV).

Jesus' followers are called to join Him in the role of serving the poor and working towards justice with Him. Bring the good news that death and sin have been defeated and be the good news that releases resources to the most needy. Church history is full of examples of this missional servanthood exemplified by ordinary Christians.

"In the fourth century, the emperor Julian launched a campaign to institute pagan charities in an effort to match the Christians. Julian complained in a letter to the high priest of Galatia in 362 that the pagans needed to equal the virtues of Christians, for recent Christian growth was caused by their 'moral character, even if pretended,' and by their 'benevolence toward strangers and care for the graves of the dead.' In a letter to another priest, Julian wrote, 'I think that when the poor happened to be neglected and overlooked by the priests, the impious Galileans observed this and devoted themselves to benevolence.' And he also wrote, 'The impious Galileans support not only their poor, but ours as well, everyone can see that our people lack aid from us.'

"Clearly, Julian loathed 'the Galileans.' He even suspected that their benevolence had ulterior motives. But he recognized that his charities and that of organized paganism paled in comparison with Christian efforts that had created 'a miniature welfare state in an empire which for the most part lacked social services' [Paul Johnson, *A History of Christianity*. New York: Atheneum, 1976: 75]. By Julian's day in the fourth century it was too late to overtake this colossal result, the seeds for which had been planted in such teachings as 'I am my brother's keeper,' 'Do unto others as you would have them do onto you,' and 'It is more blessed to give than to receive.'"[36]

"The Millennials are intensely community focused. They are more likely to be in a church where the leadership and the congregation care about and are involved in the community they serve."[37] Not only must there be clear concern about serving the community and the global poor, there need to be ways in which everyone in the church can take part in missional service. Again to quote the findings of a key study, "Young adults are more likely to stay engaged in the church if they are directly involved in the Missional activities of the church."[38]

We need to encourage all members and especially the youth to explore solutions to some of the mega-challenges of their world. This could take to the form of studying a Bible passage like Isaiah 40 together, and exploring the implications of God's creative power in the universe. As a part of His redeemed family, we can address the ongoing fractures we witness in His world and see what resources we can offer to address them. In their book *Do Something Hard: A Teenage Rebellion Against Low Expectations*, Millennial authors Alex and Brett Harris give numerous examples of ways young men and women have tackled some of society's great inequities. Sadly, in our church culture they are often allowed to do no more than spectate and cheer. Consider creating internships as opportunities for leadership development as young adults become involved in the mission of the church. We should be equipping youth and young adults for mission, giving some of them opportunities to grow as leaders, as well as a safe place to fail.

WHOLE BIBLE: Christ-Centered Home and Work Life

A holistic church is one where we have a 24/7 walk with Jesus. We enjoy the gatherings that encourage us through preaching, teaching, worship, sacraments, and fellowship. We also learn to love and serve Jesus in all areas of life. We see that Jesus is far more than simply the right answer to Sunday issues; He is the resource and power for Monday through Saturday issues. We have a confidence that the Bible speaks about Jesus as the key to the complex issues of life that range from marriage, parenting, forgiveness, environmental challenges, and to sanctity of life issues. It takes an effort together to see the implications of the cosmically potent words of a passage like Colossians 1:15-20 (NIV):

"The Son is the image of the invisible God, the firstborn over all creation. For in him all things were created: things in heaven and on earth, visible and invisible, whether thrones or powers or rulers or authorities; all things have been created through him and for him. He is before all things, and in him all things hold together. And he is the head of the body, the church; he is the beginning and the firstborn from among the dead, so that in everything he might have the supremacy. For God was pleased to have all his fullness dwell in him, and through him to reconcile to himself all things, whether things on earth or things in heaven, by making peace through his blood, shed on the cross."

As we think about a future church, we know changes need to be made, and these are not simply pandering after a spoiled generation, in the popular sense of the word. Instead, we must honestly explore what deficits need addressing and consult the Lord of the Church for wisdom on how to do so. This involves developing a robust Christian worldview by which we can meet all of life. "Millennials need guidance on engaging culture meaningfully, and from a distinctly Christian perspective. This idea of finding a way to bring their faith in Jesus to the problems they encounter in the world seems to be one of the most powerful motivations of today's practicing Christian Millennials."[39]

Tim Keller in his book, *Every Good Work*, addresses this holistic church issue, explaining how this Christian worldview enables a whole view of life. He writes:

"To be a Christian in business, then, means much more than just being honest or not sleeping with your coworkers. It even means more than personal evangelism or holding a Bible study at the office. Rather, it means thinking out the implications of the gospel worldview and God's purposes for your whole work life— and for the whole of the organization under your influence... So when we say that Christians work from a gospel worldview, it does not mean that they are constantly speaking about Christian teaching in their work. Some people think of the gospel as something we are principally to 'look at' in our work. This would mean that Christian musicians should play Christian music, Christian writers should write stories about conversion, and Christian businessmen and -women should work for companies that make Christian-themed products and services for Christian customers. Yes, some Christians in those fields would sometimes do well to do those things, but it is a mistake to think that the Christian worldview is operating only when we are doing such overtly Christian activities. Instead, think of the gospel as a set of glasses through which you 'look' at everything else in the world. Christian artists, when they do this faithfully, will not be completely beholden either to profit or to naked self-expression; and they will tell the widest variety of stories. Christians in business will see profit as only one of several bottom lines; and they will work passionately for any kind of enterprise that serves the common good. The Christian writer can constantly be showing the destructiveness of making something besides God into the central thing, even without mentioning God directly."[40]

CONCLUSION: God Confidence:

At the end of the day, we must fix our gaze on Him who is the author and finisher of our faith (Heb. 12:2). Otherwise, we may well grow discouraged, cynical, or proud. Thankfully, we have a living Lord who longs to work with those whose hearts are turned toward Him. He forgives our failings and can guide us to overcome our blindness. He is committed to the future of His Church and reminds us that nothing can thwart the advance of His Church. Ultimately, our confidence is in Christ Jesus and His Word, not techniques, statistics, and demographics, or the latest fad of church. He is our hope and confidence for the future.

"You cannot find excellent corporate worship until you stop trying to find excellent corporate worship and pursue God himself."[41]

Discussion Questions

1. Is enough focus given to a maturing spiritual life in church? Give examples. Suggest some solutions. What has been helpful to you in growing spiritually?

2. Is there a "clear pathway" in our churches that can be chosen for spiritual formation? Discuss how that might be improved over the coming twelve months.

3. Reflect with others on the concept of a "Holistic Church", where are you encouraged and where do we need to work harder?

4. 4. Try the suggested study of Isaiah 40 together. List the things it tells about God's nature and activities. Look for the promises that are given to us. Think together about two or three critical issues your church community can address around it and explore connections that could begin to be made.

Notes

[1] See Ephesians 3:10ff

[2] Michael Green, *The Message of Matthew: The Kingdom of Heaven*, The Bible Speaks Today (Leicester, England; Downers Grove, IL: InterVarsity Press, 2001), 178.

[3] Ibid., 180.

[4] Paul Farmer, *Haiti After the Earthquake* (New York: PublicAffairs, 2011), 360-361.

[5] Rev. Peter Brierley, *Church Leader*, Seminar content by the Evangelical Alliance, U.K.

[6] Demographers differ on dates but these are generally accepted.

[7] Kathleen Shaputis, *The Crowded Nest Syndrome: Surviving the Return of Adult Children* (Olympia, WA: Clutter Fairy Publishing, 2003).

[8] "Generations in Canada": http://www12.statcan.ca/census-recensement/2011/as-sa/98-311-x/98-311-x2011003_2-eng.cfm

[9] Sources: The Huffington Post | By Posted: 11/05/2013. Author Dale Schwabel – Gen Y expert (29 yrs old).

[9] About 9 million.

[9] Mark Prensky, http://marcprensky.com ,MCB University Press (accessed November 6, 2013).

[9] David Kinnaman, *You Lost Me: Why Young Christians Are Leaving Church...and Rethinking Faith* (Grand Rapids: Baker Books, 2011).

[9] Ibid.

[9] Hemorrhaging Faith, 101.

[9] Rev. John Stott

[9] Rachel Evans, *CNN Blog*, 2013

[9] *USA Today* interview April 12, 2012

[9] --http://www.plainsimplefaith.com/2013/05/this-is-why-my-generation-is-leaving-the-church/

[9] Christian Smith, Melina Lundquist Denton, *Soul Searching: The Religious and Spiritual Lives of American Teenagers* Oxford University Press, 2005,; 2009 reprint

[9] *Millennial Author Rachel Evans on CNN 2013*

[9] Rachel Held Evans, *Evolving in Monkey Town: How a Girl Who Knew All The Answers Learned to Ask the Questions* (Grand Rapids, MI: Zondervan, 2010).

[9] Hemorrhaging Faith, 114.

[10] About 9 million.

[11] Mark Prensky, http://marcprensky.com ,MCB University Press (accessed November 6, 2013).

[12] David Kinnaman, *You Lost Me: Why Young Christians Are Leaving Church...and Rethinking Faith* (Grand Rapids: Baker Books, 2011).

[13] Ibid.

[14] Hemorrhaging Faith, 101.

[15] Rev. John Stott

[16] Rachel Evans, *CNN Blog,* 2013

[17] *USA Today* interview April 12, 2012

[18]--http://www.plainsimplefaith.com/2013/05/this-is-why-my-generation-is-leaving-the-church/

[19] Christian Smith, Melina Lundquist Denton, *Soul Searching: The Religious and Spiritual Lives of American Teenagers* Oxford University Press, 2005,; 2009 reprint

[20] *Millennial Author Rachel Evans on CNN 2013*

[21] Rachel Held Evans, *Evolving in Monkey Town: How a Girl Who Knew All The Answers Learned to Ask the Questions* (Grand Rapids, MI: Zondervan, 2010).

[22] Hemorrhaging Faith, 114.

[23] I am indebted to Dr. Krish Kandiah's lectures at Regent College (June 2013) for the root ideas expressed here.

[24] Ephesians 2:8-10

[25] Dietrich Bonhoeffer, *The Cost of Discipleship.*

[26] Dallas Willard

[27] Luke 9:23ff, Matthew 16:24

[28] Wright, After You Believe: Why Christian Character Matters, 2010, HarperOne

[29]

[30] -http://thomrainer.com/2013/12/11/six-ways-millennials-are-shaping-the-church/ - accessed: 5/30/14

[31] Hemorrhaging Faith 111.

[32] Stark, *The Rise of Christianity, 161.*

[33] Hemorrhaging Faith

[34] Rainer, *I Am a Church Member.*

[35] A term popularized by Alvin Toffler in his bestselling 1970 book *Future Shock.*

[36] Stark, *The Rise of Christianity.*

[37] Thom Rainer: http://thomrainer.com/2013/12/11/six-ways-mi llennials-are-shaping-the-church/

[38] Hemorrhaging Faith, page 113

[39] https://www.barna.org/barna-update/millennials/635-5-reasons-millennials-stay-connected-to-church#.Ut6_v_bTnq0

[40] Timothy Keller, *Every Good Endeavor.*

[41] Carson, D. A. Worship by the Book. Grand Rapids, MI: Zondervan, 2002. Print.

Gandalf Gets the Final Word

In *The Lord Of The Rings*, the wise sage Gandalf writes a letter to a young pilgrim Bilbo; in it he includes a poem that is to remind him of lasting truths that matter when on a journey that will have many challenges. Its message is very pertinent when thinking about the Church. Here are the lines of the poem that Tolkien records from the pen of Gandalf:

> *All that is gold does not glitter,*
> *Not all those who wander are lost;*
> *The old that is strong does not wither,*
> *Deep roots are not reached by the frost.*
> *From the ashes a fire shall be woken,*
> *A light from the shadows shall spring;*
> *Renewed shall be blade that was broken,*
> *The crownless again shall be king.*[1]

Here are a few lessons that can be gleaned from the words of Gandalf's poem. There is gold to be found and, it is priceless! The church is God's great and wonderful idea for a renewed community on earth, and when properly formed and enjoyed, it can be golden. The church was not a later invention that people thought up, nor was it an afterthought; it was always central to the saving mission of Jesus and the outcome of His triumph. Paul affirms this to be true in his Ephesian letter "to bring to light for everyone what is the plan of the mystery hidden for ages in God who created all things, so that through the church the manifold wisdom of God might now be made known to the rulers and authorities in the heavenly places."[2] The church is the result of the good news of Jesus' coming into the world and gathering people who respond to his invitation. Through the church God will bless the world and display His infinite wisdom. "So then, as the gospel spreads throughout the world, this new and variegated Christian community develops. It is as if a great drama is being enacted. History is the theatre, the world is the stage, and church members in every land are the actors. God himself has written the play, and he directs and produces it. Act by act, scene by scene, the story continues to unfold."[3] Who would want to settle for less – being an active part of the church is a dimension of the gold of God's free grace.

However as Gandalf's poem says, "all that is gold does not glitter." In our desire to find and experience authenticity in the church, we will find truth in these words. The tempting *glittery paths* of contemporary church life in our culture may not lead to gold, but it is out there to be found. There are many fashionable expressions of churches across the land that have either lost their message, and therefore their power, or that have a lot of glitter, e.g. big programs, bands and smoke machines, but very little gold. Resist getting stuck or allured by these and seek earnestly to find a fellowship of believers who are focused on

Jesus, supporting one another and serving His mission in the world.

Don't be discouraged if it takes time to find such a church because, "Not all those who wander are lost". We may seem to wander off the path of what is considered mainstream church activity, yet we may not be lost, but getting closer to authentic church life. In fact, we may need to choose to abandon the path of the well-known places to discover places of rest, engagement, shalom and fruitfulness. Too much emphasis can be placed on attending a service and passively watching the performance, or routinely going through a liturgy of worship and yet not having genuinely engaged in being a church. Do not despair, continue to wander, all the while looking for those who are sincere about serving their master and joining with those who are doing the same.

As we have seen in the forgoing chapters, there are ancient paths that have been trod which enable a Christian and authentic churches to stay empowered and engaged. These paths are the tried and true spiritual disciplines that feed the soul, break with the past, and crucify the flesh. It will be tempting to go after every new and novel fad that comes along in the church, but many of these will be found to be little more than passing trends and, in fact, sidetracks. Our challenge will be to stay to the old ways in which God's people have historically met with their Lord and one another in the Word, in Worship, and sharing in witness. Again from Gandalf's poem:

"...*The old that is strong does not wither,*
Deep roots are not reached by the frost."

We may encounter places of withering and frost, but we persist because we have a profound hope that we will discover in the emerging light and renewing blade, the splendor of the King and His kingdom.

In closing, we change the metaphor from journeying as in Gandalf's poem to the image of farming. Paul closes his words to the early church in Galatia with the encouragement to keep sowing good seed through the word, their witness, and good works, knowing that doing so will lead to a harvest. We too are called to sow in obedience and do so with those around us following Christ, knowing that we will get to be a part of a great harvest.

"So let's not allow ourselves to get fatigued doing good. At the right time we will harvest a good crop if we don't give up, or quit. Right now, therefore, every time we get the chance, let us work for the benefit of all, starting with the people closest to us in the community of faith." Galatians 6:9-10 The Message

Church: Is There An App For That?

What an age we live in! There are some amazing apps that make short work of undertakings that, in the past, were very complex. As already noted in the preface of this book, there are now hundreds of thousands of apps that can do a stunning array of things. A recent article highlighted some of the more unusual tasks that can be performed by these simple low-cost apps.[4]

Here are some claims of a few recent offerings:

- WordLens – "Point the camera at a foreign language (on a menu, say) and it turns into English on the screen. Spanish-only at the moment; more languages promised."

- NASA – "News from Nasa. Find out when you'll be able to see the International Space Station passing. Also videos, images and lots of info on planets and asteroids and comets."

- Flipboard – "Dubbed the next generation of magazine publishing, Flipboard takes news feeds from various sites, including Twitter and Facebook, and brings them together beautifully."

- IA Writer – "...It's word-processing stripped back and fans swear their productivity has improved as a result."

- Real Tools – "Leave the weighty toolbox behind, with 18 tools crammed into one little app – everything from a ruler to a spirit level, and all surprisingly accurate."

- Evernote – "Create a searchable, tag-able database of all the web-clippings, photos and notes you need to hand wherever you are. Syncs to every device imaginable."

No doubt, there must be an app for reviewing the array of the latest and most innovative apps! However, when it comes to the church, there are no quick shortcuts. There is no switch to flip or button to highlight. Instead, we find that Jesus invites us to join him on a lifelong journey. One which will involve great change, great challenge, and great rewards. Because he is making those who follow him into a community that resembles his glorious likeness, there will be required of those undertaking the adventure, a persistent obedience that will mean no short-cuts, no apps, and no resistance. However, the promise and hope that all who are a part of His church journey with, is the ultimate destiny of that company. The apostle John saw and wrote about in the last chapter of Revelation;

I saw Heaven and earth new-created. Gone the first Heaven, gone the first earth, gone the sea.

2 I saw Holy Jerusalem, new-created, descending resplendent out of Heaven, as ready for God as a bride for her husband.

3-5 I heard a voice thunder from the Throne: "Look! Look! God has moved into the neighborhood, making his home with men and women! They're his people, he's their God. He'll wipe every tear from their eyes. Death is gone for good—tears gone, crying gone, pain gone—all the first order of things gone." The Enthroned continued, "Look! I'm making everything new. Write it all down—each word dependable and accurate."

6-8 Then he said, "It's happened. I'm A to Z. I'm the Beginning, I'm the Conclusion. From Water-of-Life Well I give freely to the thirsty. Conquerors inherit all this. I'll be God to them, they'll be sons and daughters to me.

Revelation 21:1-8 (The Message Version)

Notes

1 J. R. R. Tolkien, The Fellowship of The Ring.

2 *The Holy Bible: English Standard Version* (Wheaton: Standard Bible Society, 2001). Ephesians 3:9,10

3 John R. W. Stott, *God's New Society: The Message of Ephesians*, The Bible Speaks Today (Downers Grove, IL: InterVarsity Press, 1979), 123–124.

4http://www.theguardian.com/technology/2010/dec/26/best-apps-iphone-ipad-android

CPSIA information can be obtained at www.ICGtesting.com
Printed in the·USA
LVOW04s2152090415

433939LV00021B/324/P